1

EBDON TO CHARLERY

LONDON ROAD LEGENDS

By JAMIE JONES

EBDON TO CHARLERY : LONDON ROAD LEG-
ENDS
COPYRIGHT: JAMIE JONES 2011
All Rights Reserved

ISBN: 978-0-9571122-0-9

First Published 2011 by
DIVISIONFOUR PUBLISHING
Peterborough, England

"Ebdon to Charlery. He's in with a chance, he's into the area…..HE'S DONE IT, Ken Charlery, 89 minutes".

Foreword

As heroes and legends go, my first venture into this world of dreams was as a six year old when I was bought a Superman outfit for my birthday and proceeded to terrorise my family for the next three months with deeds of daring and nonsense... well, it seemed like a good idea at the time.

As the years rolled by (and excluding a young Debbie Harry) my next ledge was to be the magnificent and majestic Kenny Dalglish MBE. I could bang on for hours about this man but the following stats tell their own story: At Anfield he won seven league titles, three European Cups and five domestic cups, he is still Scotland's most capped and leading scorer and ... at Celtic he won four Scottish First Division titles, four Scottish Cups and one Scottish League Cup with the club, halcyon days.

Anyway ... this Posh Legends book is to be a trip down memory lane, and I have been kindly invited to preface what I am sure will be an excellent dose of nostalgia and unbiased opinion. As my tenure at our football club has been relatively short I will keep my legend view the same.

'The Trinity' ... Mclean, Mackail-Smith and Boyd, a trio of young, hungry and talented individuals we plucked from the world of non-league football and who now perform just one step away from the promised land of the Premiership. There are plenty of other players who have performed outstandingly for the club whilst I have been at London Road but I would need a book of my own if I started.

These young men came, saw and conquered and they would all tell you it was due to the lads they played with, so I will add modesty and integrity to their talents.

Short and sweet ... keep it Posh.

Darragh MacAnthony

Introduction

I am only 35 years old, but my memory is fading fast. I have an irrational fear that when my son grows up, I won't be able to tell him about the legends that have graced London Road, because I won't remember. Just in case it does happen, I thought I had better write this book.

I hope it gives the reader an insight into players from the past, the present and provokes some smiles of recognition. There is a slight bias towards players from the late 80s onwards but that's when I started watching Posh. So I'm sorry if I've left your favourite player out. I would like to thank all of those that have contributed to, or purchased the book, as well as Darragh for writing the foreword and Mitch for keeping the project moving forward.

So this book is dedicated to my son, Harrison – a book that shows him just some of the amazing players that have played for "Dad's Posh". I hope that we get to watch many more special players grace the London Road turf in the years to come.

Up The Posh
Jamie

Norman Rigby

1951-1962
Appearances: 436
Goals: 4

Looking at the old black & white photographs of Norman Rigby he appears to have stepped straight out of the pages of the Hotspur comic. He is the epitome of the no-nonsense post-war defender; uncompromising, Brylcreemed hair, granite jaw and and unwavering stare.

After joining the club in 1951 Norman was variously a player, coach and manager at Posh over the next 20 years. He began his career at Notts County and was signed by Bob Gurney who made him captain. His 11 years as skipper were marked by unprecedented success and the establishment of Peterborough United's reputation as one of the great FA Cup giant-killing teams of the era. Norman led the team to five successive Midland League titles and election to the Football League he Norman played over 40 games, at the age of 37, as Posh convincingly won the Fourth Division championship and watched by more than 15,000 fans he collected the Fourth

Division championship trophy before Posh proceeded to round off their record-breaking season with a six goal victory over Barrow.

Norman played a handful of league games in Division Three during the 1961-62 campaign before joining Boston United and playing for a further two seasons. He returned to London Road as Posh trainer/coach during 1964 and was appointed caretaker manager in September 1967 following the resignation of Gordon Clark.

Despite the scandal – some might say travesty - of Posh being found guilty of financial irregularities in November 1967 and demoted to the Fourth Division Norman accepted the manager's job on a permanent basis. Although the team had little more to play for than personal pride, his skill as a motivator ensured that Posh battled to the end and finished in a respectable ninth place in Division Three. Norman resigned as manager in January 1969, his two main achievements while in charge being the signing of two future Posh greats Jim Hall and Tommy Robson.

Ellis Stafford

1954-1963
Appearances: 215
Goals: 9

Ellis Stafford is one of the great characters in Peterborough United's history and had a long and happy association with the club. Writing after his death in 2007 Evening Telegraph Chief Sports Writer Alan Swann described him as "that rare breed of footballer. He was loved by his team-mates, fans and even his opponents didn't have a bad word to say about him." He joined from Scarborough in 1954 and went on to make over 200 appearances for Posh with the bulk of those coming in the Midland League. In 1964 Ellis left London Road to join Corby Town but soon returned to Posh and for the next 20 years was employed as Commercial and Pools Manager at the club.

Ellis started his career with Posh as a centre forward but was soon converted into a half-back. During his time with Posh, Ellis played in every position except centre half and, in the days before substitutes were allowed, played in goal as stand-in for an injured goalkeeper. Ellis scored eight goals during his spell with Posh and was rewarded for his long service with a benefit game against Newcastle United in May 1959.

In 2007 Ellis recalled his time at Posh in an interview with club historian Peter Lane; "In those days, even though we were a non-league side, we trained as hard as any Football League club.

"They were enjoyable times at Peterborough. At the time I was paid between £18 and £25 a week, which wasn't that bad in those days. It was certainly better than 'working for a living'. He singled out Dennis Emery as the best player he has ever played; "Dennis was simply brilliant. There is no other way to describe him. He was the best player I played with for sure.

'My favourite match was when we played Sheffield Wednesday in the fourth round of the FA Cup back in 1961. I was born in Sheffield and over 50,000 fans packed into Hillsborough to see the game. We were very unfortunate to lose 2-0, but it was a great experience. I also thoroughly enjoyed our first match in the Football League in 1960 when we defeated Wrexham 3-0. It was a great day at London Road and one I will always remember."

Denis Emery

1954 – 1963
Appearances: 308
Goals: 231

The finest player ever to pull on a Posh shirt? Many think so. Whether you agree or not, Denis was a quality footballer and, if he were around today, there is no doubt whatsoever he would be playing in the Premiership, probably with a top club, and on the fringes of, if not in, the national side. Yes – he was that good. So - why did it never happen? Well - like with the Manchester United team a few years earlier – it was down to fate.

Denis Emery joined the Posh in 1954. When he left, nine years later, he had over 300 appearances and 200 goals to his credit. Incredible statistics, by today's standards, for Denis was a scheming inside forward rather than an out and out striker. Not only that but, like Bobby Charlton and Stanley Matthews, all his skill was in his feet. His heading ability was, um, marginal, but that's not important. His elegance as a player had to be seen to be appreciated. I may have been young then but I was old enough to understand that not everyone could cover ground effortlessly and switch the play from one wing to the other with one 40-yard pinpoint pass. I count myself lucky that I was able to watch Denis do it. He made it look so easy, I thought I could be as good. Guess what? I was wrong.

Denis had been at Peterborough for around seven years and although we'd made the Football League and the Third Division, there were surely better things to come for him. But basically, it all ended the day of the FA Cup second round second replay against Colchester. Denis had scored a late equaliser in the first replay, so the second replay was at a neutral ground - Carrow Road. Denis was travelling to London Road for the team coach when his car was in collision with a lorry. He was badly injured, critically injured.

At school, we knew nothing of this. We got out at 4 o'clock, straight on to the supporter's club coach and off to Norwich we went. It wasn't until we got there that we heard of the car crash, and even then we had no idea how bad it was – we were only concerned with plastering 'UP THE POSH' stickers all over the town, including a couple on the glass doors of Anglia TV. Perhaps they're still there but I digress. We won the game in the first half with three goals from George Hudson, so we all went home happy, not realising what a black day it had really been.

Slowly, Denis recovered and yes, he played again. When he scored his first goal - an elegant chip of a free kick - I remember the whole team rushed up to congratulate him. But it wasn't the start of a great comeback. Denis was never the same again. The physical legacy of his injuries meant he just couldn't do it any more, not the way he used to. He was sold to Bedford for a nominal sum, so much for sentiment in football.

Sadly, Denis was never to fully recover from his injuries, and died as a direct result of them in 1986. He was 52. Gone – but never to be forgotten. Not as long as there is a Posh fan alive.

Rob Brown
This article was first published in the fanzine Blue Moon

Our Dennis

Tall with unruly golden blonde hair. Thin, long-legged, precocious, enigmatic and talented, oceans of talent. Most of us recognised that he was a special player on first viewing but some were still sceptical as he didn't look like a stereotypical 50's footballer.

Until his arrival we had not won the Midland League but Denis' arrival transformed the team. His elegant style, powerful finishing and accurate passing made him stand out. In an era when brutally uncompromising tacking was the norm Denis side-stepped it all and often left the pitch without a fleck of mud on his shorts. At one time he made 185 consecutive appearances which showed how fit and robust he was.

His opponents left the pitch exasperated as he stroked the ball around the pitch and moved with the grace of a ballet dancer. His long thin legs didn't look strong enough but the sight of goal lent his shooting venom. 231 goals in 308 starts was proof enough oh his appetite for goals.

After election to the Football League it was seemingly inevitable that Denis should have the honour of scoring our fist League goal. In that first season Denis contributed 17 goals in 52 League and Cup games but more importantly laid on a large proportion of the chances that allowed terry Bly to score 52 goals in 46 League games.

The big clubs, among them Arsenal and Spurs, were said to be interested but Denis remained loyal to Posh. Rumour has it that he turned down a move to Spurs as they wanted him to dress in a suit and not the Teddy Boy outfit he turned up in.

I cried, as many did, on hearing of his accident. A light had gone out, that skill, that perfect passing and that wry smile as he left the pitch another victory in the bag. The elegance, the swagger and the toss of his hair. Easy going he liked a beer on occasion and hated training if it involved too much running.

One final memory. Occasionally, on an afternoon off work I would go and watch the players training. At the end of one session after some discussion a couple of players placed a pound note each underneath a stone. Denis placed a football on the junction of the halfway line and touch line in front of the main stand. He then took a couple of steps and hit the ball in the direction of the corner flag at the London Road End (in front of what is now the Medical/Police Centre). He did this 10 times and hit the flag direct eight times. Then he picked up the money and with a smile went down the tunnel.

Denis was the man who guided Peterborough United in to the footballing consciousness of the nation and in nine great years made Peterborough United, Posh. I still see him every time I go to London Rd. There he is on the pitch standing tall on those long elegant legs just being Denis Emery, my total Posh hero.

Brian Seaton

Terry Bly

1960-1962

Appearances: 101

Goals: 87

81-88. Those numbers mean anything to you? No, that's not when he lived. As any Posh fan knows, that's his League scoring record. 81 goals in 88 appearances. Oh, yes - it's easy for you to scoff now and say that things were different in those days. Defenders were crap, goalies were rubbish, it was much easier to score, and no record set then should be given any credence whatsoever. Sod you, then. Stop reading now. Oh – so you didn't stop. Ah! So you do want to know about a goal-scoring phenomenon, after all? Ok, then.

Terry Bly came to us from Norwich in 1960, just in time for the most famous debut season ever in the history of the Football League. I still don't know how we got him. Norwich had been a force to be reckoned with the previous season, and had reached the semi-final of the FA Cup with the help of Bly's goals. Jimmy Hagan was our manager at the time, and obviously somehow persuaded him that his future was at

London Road rather than in Division One. Good for him.

So – it's 1960, and we're in the League at last. And what a team we have! By the end of the season, that team has scored 134 goals and Bly has a personal tally of 52! Ha! No – it's not a joke. What it is is a post-war record that still stands. Maybe it always will.

Terry Bly was an old fashioned centre forward before it was out of fashion. Strong in the air and a real hustler on the ground. Hence there were as many scrambled goals as great goals, but they all counted. Sadly, I can only remember seeing the last three – the ones that set the record – in the home game against Barrow at the end of that fantastic season.

Terry Bly is modest about his achievements, believing that anyone could have played centre forward in that team because the likes of Emery, Hails and McNamee provided so many chances for him. Bloody rubbish, Terry! However good the team was, the chances still had to be put away, and there's never been a better converter since John the Baptist. It couldn't last for ever, though. In hindsight, it didn't last long at all – just a couple of years.

Much to my (and a lot of others) disappointment, Terry Bly was transferred to Coventry in 1962, where

Jimmy Hill was developing the Sky Blues into a formidable team which was to become our arch enemy in the Third Division promotion race. Bly stayed there for a couple of years, netting 26 times in 32 games, before he was replaced by another Posh centre forward, George Hudson. He moved to Notts County, where a serious knee injury more or less ended his league career. He turned non-league, to Grantham Town, as a player/manager, but he wasn't finished – far from it. By the time he retired, in 1970, he had scored 125 goals in 199 appearances. And he didn't stop there, as he continued to manage the club for another 8 years, clocking up over 700 games in charge!

Terry Bly lived in Grantham up until his death in 2009, so don't let any twat tell you that Margaret Thatcher is the town's most famous person. Next time you get that as a quiz question, you'll know the answer.

Rob Brown
This article was first published in the fanzine Blue Moon

Derek Dougan

1963 -1965

Appearances: 90

Goals: 46

ADD spells 'add'. Oh, yes. But ADD stands for Alexander Derek Dougan. And that spells 'Legend'. A Posh legend. Also, incidentally, a legend at Aston Villa, Leicester and Wolves. But not always for the right reasons.

Born on 20th January 1938, Dougan was brought to Peterborough in 1963 from Aston Villa by manager Gordon Clarke for a club record fee of £25,000. He'd already been at Portsmouth and Blackburn, so he'd moved about a bit. I remember hearing he was on the transfer list at Villa and thinking 'Wow! If only we could get him here!' Never thought it would happen.

Dougan was already a proven striker – not that we called 'em that, then – a big name, but with a certain reputation. At the Villa, he'd shaved his head. No big deal now but, in those days, it marked him out as a bit of a rebel. Maybe big clubs were scared of him. Maybe they thought he was trouble. He certainly was to Third Division defences!

He was also an instant hero at London Road and was immediately christened 'The Doog'. Junior Posh fans (of whom I was one) worshipped him. He was always friendly, always ready for a few words and always happy to scrawl his autograph on any grubby scrap of paper that we kids used to thrust at him.

On the pitch, there were many highlights in his relatively short Posh career. During the great Cup Run of 1964/5, we played Chesterfield. Unluckily for them, their centre-half was well past his sell-by-date and the Doog had a field day. We won 3-0, thanks to his hat-trick of headers. Like most of the travelling Posh fans, I was behind the goal where he scored them all... 'Dooo-gan, Dooo-gan, DOOO – GAN!!'

And, of course, there was the equaliser against Arsenal. He beat Ian Ure, Arsenal's Scottish International centre-half, and slid the ball past Burns, the goalie. Not his greatest goal, but one of his most important. Apparently, the roar that followed was heard as far away as Newborough.

Doog always celebrated his goals with right arm aloft, curling over his head. The Posh Post, the club's newspaper of the time, carried a picture of his son, still in nappies, who he'd taught to do the same thing. Sweet, eh?

There used to be a story which told of the time the Doog met Pat Jennings in the street - Dougan nodded and the goalie dived in the gutter! Ah, the old ones are the best. Mind you, the Doog could be difficult. One time he was receiving treatment just off the pitch behind the goal line. We were attacking. Suddenly the referee blew his whistle. Everyone stopped, puzzled. What had he blown for? The ref pointed to Dougan. He was sitting with one foot just touching the goal line. Yes, he'd given the Doog's foot offside! Treatment forgotten, Dougan leapt up, sprinted after the ref and remonstrated with him. Yes – I think remonstrated is the word. Today, he'd have got a straight red for dissent, but things were different then, my boys...

Different was certainly the word for his heading ability, and that leads on to one of my favourite memories. Posh made a move down the right wing and a cross came whipping over, high and hard. Too high? Too hard? No. With a mighty leap, the Doog met it somewhere near the penalty spot. I estimate he was about six feet off the ground. Next second, the ball had smacked against the bar, bounced once and gone out of play on the touchline. The goalie never moved. I swear he was shaking more than the cross-bar, and we were surprised the goal didn't fall down. I've never seen a more powerful header, and I've seen a few.

It wasn't just Doog's strength that was important, though – his delicate flicks set up many a goal for his striking partners. For a big man he was also quite amazingly agile on the ground and had the speed to match. Speed, strength, control, what more could you want? But that was the problem, you see. We were never going to keep him, were we? He was a class player, and he wasn't going to languish in Division 3 for long. In 1965 he was transferred to Leicester, and a year or so later to Wolves, where he made his reputation and stayed until his retirement in 1975, after nearly 300 appearances.

As one of the directors, Harold Trelfa, said to me at a supporters meeting a year or so after he left, 'Dougan was a luxury we couldn't afford.' Well, maybe so. But – what the hell it was great while it lasted, and Derek Dougan has lasted well, too.

Outspoken enough to be the Chairman of the PFA in the 70's, and he remained a rebel until his death in 2007. He even appeared on Question Time as a spokesman for the UK Independence Party. The Doog

– he's an independent, all right. And look, you Wolves fans – he was OUR hero first, OK?

Rob Brown
This article was first published in the fanzine Blue Moon

The Doog

'The Doog' was my very first boyhood footballing hero. I would be about 10 or 11 years old when he joined Posh. He was tall and gangly, with bandy legs and he sort of flapped his arms by his side when he ran, which gave him a really distinctive look. Despite all that, he seemed to glide rather than run.

Being at a very impressionable age, for some reason I began modelling my own footballing movements on his. I developed the bandy run and the flappy arms and my parents were becoming increasingly concerned. Thankfully this phase soon passed, as I couldn't quite pull off "that Doog look" - I was more Max Wall than Derek Dougan.

It's funny how little incidents from a match stick with you for life. One of our players knocked a long ball down the wing, but over-hit it and everyone gave it up for a goal-kick. Even the opposing defenders had turned away and were setting themselves up for a goal-kick, but The Doog hared after this ball as it was heading for the corner flag. Everyone looked at each other wondering what the fuck he was doing, but he'd obviously spotted something that no-one else had.

This is where the years haven't been kind to my memory, but the ball either stopped in a puddle or rolled into the base of the corner flag - I can't remember which. It was obviously still in play and Dougan must have had an idea that might happen when he set off after it. The funniest thing was seeing all the other players - especially the defenders - suddenly wake up and go belting after him when he came away with the ball. I'd like to think that he then took the ball round the 'keeper and slotted it just inside the near post, but I don't think he did.

He wasn't here that long, but any of my generation will tell you what a legend he was. In the days when men had haircuts rather than hairstyles and picked one and had it for life, The Doog was one of the first footballers to have a range of hairstyles - including a shaven head years before it became so ubiquitous -

and he just always seemed so 'cool' to me. But underneath was an Irish temper - the crowd knew that he was never far away from letting rip and we all loved that edginess about him.

A brilliant header of the ball with lovely feet and an intelligent footballer - I believe he was one of the early PFA representatives, although that sort of thing meant nothing to me at that age. There may have been better players at Posh over the years (but I can't think of too many) and longer-serving ones, but he was special. The term 'legend' is over-used, but how many Posh players do you know who were ever called "The" something?

Bob Laughton

Chris Turner

1969-1978
Appearances: 357
Goals: 42

When you are young your sporting hero should be a colossus. He should be a rock, a giant of a man and someone who you regard as the toughest man around. Christopher James Turner or as he will always be known to Posh fans, Son of God, was that man to me.

As a football mad 13 year old who fell in love with Posh when we were truly truly awful and languishing at the bottom of the whole football league Chris was to me the player that stood out week in week out. He was the player I wanted to be when I grew up (if I ever have) and along with Sir Tommy Robson was the reason I made my parents lives a misery if, leading up to a home game there was even a chance that I wouldn't be going to London Road.

It is ironic that the first visit Chris made to London Road was as an Arsenal fan in 1965 when he saw his favourites get beaten 2-1 by the club whose history he would eventually be such a massive part of.

Chris joined Posh in 1968 leaving his home town of St Neots and a job in a paper mill to earn £6 per week as an apprentice. Norman Rigby was the manager who invited him to join the club although it was Jim Iley who gave him his chance as a professional offering him a contract in November 1969 - despite the generally held opinion Jim actually did do some good for Posh after all.

The story goes that to improve his heading ability Chris would stay behind after training heading away crosses put in by his great friend Tommy Robson. The rumours that Robbo would try and get a penalty from the wings in those sessions have always been denied.

In the season 72-73 he made the number 5 shirt his own playing in all League and Cup games. The arrival of his mentor Noel Cantwell inspired Chris who in the 73/74 Championship winning season missed only two games captaining the team and leading a defence that only conceded 38 goals during the campaign.

In 'that game' against Gillingham on Wednesday May 1st 1974 which secured the title he scored a great headed goal. It was with great pride that Chris held the trophy aloft and he has often said that the game that night was his favourite in all his time with the club.

The next season he once again played in every game and even decided to show the forwards a thing or two by scoring ten goals. Eventually, and after the heartbreak of the draw at Wrexham and bloody Dai Davies, Chris decided that it was time for him to leave the club, something he found hard to do but after turning down numerous offers over the years the club agreed to his request. 357 games plus 7 as a sub with a grand total of 43 goals was Chris' record which is only stats, none of that shows what a superb player he was.

Chris went on to have a great career especially in the fledgling professional league in America where he starred for the New England Tea Men. He was selected for the All Stars team and played alongside the likes of Pele, Beckenbauer and Cruyff - not quite Jolly Jack but not bad.

In January 1991 with the club in a mess, after the disastrous management of Mark Lawrenson and Dave Booth the club needed a manager with a Posh link, someone who was strong enough to tackle the numerous problems at the club. Chris Turner was that man.

A win in his first game away at Walsall was followed by a draw at Halifax. The best was still to come and arrived with a win against the promotion chasing Wobbs. They were despatched with a well deserved lack of respect after a great Mick Halsall goal. (Actually I can't remember the goal but any goal against them is great)

After a miraculous post-January period promotion was achieved with a draw at Chesterfield. Being two down after 19 minutes was a mere hiccup and over 5000 Posh fans celebrated with players on the pitch after the game.

The achievement of the manager emulated that of his mentor and in all his interviews subsequently when talking about his successes he was always mindful to pay respect to the influence of Noel Cantwell.

Those present were of course delirious but none of us could have thought this amazing day would soon be bettered. The next season, as well as doing well in the League saw the mighty Posh have a great run in the Rumblelows Cup and eventually faced Liverpool at home. A Gary Kimble goal saw an historic Posh win and the reputation of big Chris grew but only to those outside PUFC, we all knew already the man was a genius.

As good as we thought that night was then even better was to follow, truth be known it is doubtful anyone there that night could imagine what was to come. A run from December the 20th to March 21st saw Posh play 21, win 15 including 9 on the bounce , draw 5 and lose just 1 game.

With typically astute signings like Bobby Barnes, Tony Adcock and a hitherto unknown Steve Cooper things were coming together and the play-offs were a distinct possibility. It all came down to the last game of the season against Brentford who would be champions with a victory.

With a fluke series of results meaning we were in the play- offs despite losing we celebrated with the Brentford supporters in the middle of the pitch.

Huddersfield were to be the opposition and history shows we never lose to Huddersfield when it really matters. Plus you wouldn't be reading this book if you didn't know what happened. If you are too young or weren't there most Posh present will tell you it was amongst the greatest nights in the clubs history, better than Wembley many said but whatever it was just brilliant. Wembley was of course amazing, the magic touch of Chris was evident for all to see and the joy on his face belied the reputation he had as misery guts.

In 1992 he fulfilled an ambition by heading a consortium that purchased the club, despite suffering ill health he returned to managerial duties for short period in 1993 though it is safe to say he wishes he hadn't! His amazing commitment to the club and his undiminished love for it was shown over subsequent years when he filled in numerous roles including Coach, Chief Executive and even Sales Manager.

As a dominant centre half, inspirational captain and manager as well as an amazing servant to our football club the history books will reflect the massive part Chris Turner has played in all things Posh.

Ask any player or member of staff who has served under him and they will tell you of the admiration, respect and downright fear they held for 'The Gaffer' and still do. He has the unconditional love of all Posh fans from those generations and should have that from every Posh fan for ever and a day.

Those that have had the pleasure of knowing the man will tell you of his dry sense of humour and his generous nature, his love of his family and his 100% determination to 'get things done'.

More than anything I remember him talking to me as a 16 year old. Away at Coventry after some crowd trouble some of us younger fans had ended up on the pitch in the interest of safety (ours that is) "Why don't you just f!*k off" were his words to me. When the lads asked me what he said of course I told them he had asked after my health.

Son of God was a truly magnificent player, an awe inspiring manager but most importantly a great man.

Adi Mowles

Jim Hall

1967-1975
Appearances: 334
Goals: 137

Contrary to popular belief his full name isn't Big Jim Hall but that is how will always be known by Posh fans. Jim was what these days we'd call an 'old-fashioned centre forward'. Strong, brave and very powerful in the air he also had a good first touch and an eye for a goal. Jim was also mobile - though he modestly disagrees with this view - but most importantly was lethal in the penalty area.

Norman Rigby signed him from Northampton Town in December 1967 and Jim proved an immediate success scoring 13 goals over the rest of the season. The following season Jim formed a formidable partnership with Peter Price and was an ever-present scoring 24 goals. The deadly duo continued their scoring exploits up to 1971-1972 when Price left the Club. Considering how poor Posh were at the time this was an incredible scoring record.

When Noel Cantwell signed John Cozens, another partnership blossomed with the goals flowing freely.

Jim helped the club to win the 4th Division Championship in 1973/74 playing 46 games and scoring 14 goals. To this day he still holds the club record of 137 goals (122 League goals and 15 Cup goals), in 329 appearances for Peterborough United plus five as substitute. This total included an incredible eight hat-tricks. On two occasions, v Oldham Athletic in 1969 and Doncaster Rovers in 1973 he scored four goals

Jim stayed for another season before Cantwell sold him back to Northampton for £4,500. There he stayed for another four years and scored 28 more goals. Jim was then loaned to Cambridge United making 24 appearances and scoring 15 goals as he helped Ron Atkinson's side to the 4th Division Championship.

And we loved Big Jim so much we have never held his success with our fiercest rivals against him. I, for one, cherish the memory of that blonde head crashing a header past yet another hapless goalkeeper

Tommy Robson

1969-1981
Appearances: 514
Goals: 129

'Tommee, Tommee Robson, Tommee Robson on the wee-ing, wee-ing, Tommee, Tommee Robson, Tommy Robson on the weeng!' Ah, I can still hear the cry echoing around the terraces of London Road. No, it's nothing to do with the toilets, you dirty beasts, and I'm not taking the piss, either.

Tommy Robson was on the wee-ing quite a few times for the Posh. 440, to be exact, not counting substitutes, and that's just in the league. Adding in all the cup competitions takes the total to over 550. Those, not unnaturally, were Posh appearance records.

It all started in 1968, when Tommy was signed by Norman Rigby from Newcastle for £20,000 – a lot of money, in those days. But then, legends don't come cheap. Robson was, and still is, a Geordie lad. You can tell that when he speaks, y'know.

I was on the pitch that great night in 1974 after we'd beaten Gillingham to claim the Division Four title. The team went up into the directors box and most of the players had a few words to say. Now, I know Tommy started off with 'Gnaw, thin.' Someday, I'll find out what it means. Couldn't understand any of the rest of it. I'm sure it was nothing to do with the accent, that speaker system was always crap. Anyway, Tommy usually let his feet do the talking.

Only slight in stature, he was big in heart, and the crowd loved him, right up to his last game in 1981. When he wasn't playing, you might have found him propping up the bar at The Goat in Frognall in the days when it was renowned for its toasted sandwiches. Tommy usually had his full back on toast.

He was nippy and fast and he could swing over those lovely hanging crosses which are just a bit too far for the keeper to come for and just made for a centre forward to head in, preferably off the underside of the bar. Jim Hall bagged a few of those, and he wasn't the only one. But Tommy wasn't just nippy, he was skilful too. He could make the opposing full back look like a carthorse. He was a crowd pleaser, y'see. And he could con a gullible referee, no problem

You think diving is a modern issue? Pah Tommy Robson could dive better than Brian Phelps. Ronaldo,

Klinsmann, whoever you think of today, none of them dive as gracefully as Tommy. It was a pleasure to watch, and even more of a pleasure was the wealth of free kicks and some very pissed off full-backs. But even when they sought revenge, Tommy was usually clever enough to skip out of the way of any real trouble.

But don't think he couldn't score goals, either. Over a hundred came his way, and he earned them all, every one, because he was always gave 100%, even when he wasn't playing well. He'd never shirk or run away and hide in the midfield.

Later, much later, I had a dream – Robson, completely white haired and old, flying down that wing, jinking this way and that, speed undiminished! I'm only sorry that Tommy lost his hair, so my dream will never become reality.

But he still plays. Oh, yes! He still turns out for charity matches and testimonials and is still very much involved with football and the Posh, captaining the Legends side – hooray! Not many have been around as long as he has and good for him, I say – he's Posh man, through and through, and we love him for it. And all this from a Northampton Town reject who scored against us on his debut for the Cobblers – whoever would have thought it?

Rob Brown

This article was first published in the fanzine Blue Moon

Noel Cantwell

1973-1977, 1986-1988

Noel Cantwell, the Messiah. Forgive the blasphemy, and I'm sure Noel was uncomfortable with it, but that is how he will always be known to Posh fans of a certain vintage. Noel arrived at Posh in 1972 and, not to put to fine a point on it, completely galvanised and changed the club.

Noel hadn't had a bad career before joining Posh so his arrival was met with quite a bit of anticipation and excitement. Born in Cork in 1932 he signed for West Ham United in September 1952 and gained his first cap for the Republic of Ireland in 1953. Noel, by then captain of The Hammers, led them to the Division Two Championship in 1957-58. Even then Noel was considered a great thinker on the game and along with team mate Malcolm Allison was a mentor to the young Bobby Moore. After making 248 appearances scoring 11 goals, Matt Busby, who was still rebuilding his team after the Munich air disaster, took Noel to Old Trafford in November 1960, for a then record fee for a full-back of £29,500. Noel's charismatic personality saw him assume the captaincy at Old Trafford and he lead them to victory in the 1963

FA Cup Final against Leicester City followed by League titles in 1965 and 1967. Noel left Old Trafford in 1967 after scoring eight goals, making 137 league and cup appearances. He also won 36 International caps for his country and scored 14 goals. He filled in at centre-forward as well as left-back and captained his side several times. As a player, Noel was known as a stylish player style for such a strong, well-built man. Noel also served as Chairman of the Professional Footballers Association. In October 1967 he took over from Jimmy Hill as manager at Coventry City. It was a tough act to follow, but Noel managed to keep the Sky Blues in the old First Division of top flight football and indeed led them to a creditable position of 6th place, enabling them to qualify for the Fairs Cup in 1969-70.

Noel Cantwell had been sacked by Coventry in March 1972 and joined Posh in October 1972. It wouldn't be too much of an exaggeration to say that he arrived at a time when Posh were at their lowest with the spectre of re-election looming as the team had recorded only one win out of 13 league games. The unlamented Jim Iley had resigned and club stalwart Jim Walker took over as caretaker manager but he had been unable to change either the mood or the results. Noel received a rapturous reception from the fans before a home game against Doncaster Rovers. The team responded with their second win of the season. Ever the shy retiring type Noel cracked open the champagne in the dressing room after the game and the renaissance had begun.

Noel didn't waste any time in re-building and fashioning his own team. Former Arsenal and Notts Forest star - John Barnwell arrived as assistant-manager and Noel entered the transfer market to pay Notts County £8,000 for striker John Cozens, followed by Eric Young from Manchester United and Keith Bradley from Aston Villa, both on loan. Posh proceeded to win 13 of their remaining League games to climb six places and avoid re-election.

The following season 1973-74, Noel fashioned the team that saw Posh crowned as 4th Division Champions. He gave 12 players free transfers and one stage had only 10 players on the books. He decided not to take a summer holiday and spent £35,000 on inspired signings such as Freddie Hill, Paul Walker, Jeff Lee and Bert Murray that he believed would gel with stalwarts like Jim Hall, Tommy Robson and Chris Turner. When asked about this strategy years later Noel said: "I signed experienced performers who I knew would be suited to life in the Fourth Division. I was interested in skill but a competitive streak was just as important to me. I settled on a squad of 20, got them organised and then enjoyed watching them play."

In a season that saw Posh unbeaten at home in the League. Posh clinched the title with an epic 4-2 home win over Gillingham, with other season highlights including 28,000 packed into London Road to see Posh take on Leeds United, when they were good, very good, in the 3rd Round of the FA Cup. So impressive had been the turnaround that Noel found himself turning down the offer of the managerial position at Athletic Bilbao.

The following season Posh consolidated their position in Division Three and in an emotional return Noel took the Posh to Old Trafford to play Manchester United in the FA Cup. The ovation he got from the home crowd almost matched their cheers for the home teams 3-1 win. Noel resigned as manager in 1977 to take up a coaching position in the USA at the New England Teamen.

In 1986 he returned for a second spell as manager, replacing the unloved John Wile, inspired the team to rise from near the bottom to finish the season in 10th position. In 1988 Noel became General Manager for one year, before quitting football for good to become a publican. After 10 years behind the bar he retired, but once again football beckoned him and he was delighted to accept a position as a scout for the England national side.

Noel passed away on 8th September 2005, after a battle against cancer. Peterborough Cathedral was packed for his funeral service, with many of his former team mates and football legends in attendance. The huge turnout was a measure of the affection and respect felt for this gregarious, warm, enthusiastic good-natured man.

Freddie Hill

Appearances: 86
Goals: 8

Freddie Hill was signed by Noel Cantwell in 1973 for what was, even in those days, a paltry fee of £5,000. A brilliant cultured passer of the ball, sturdily built, he was the complete playmaker.

Bill Shankly once described him as "the best midfielder in the country on his day" and here he was playing for Posh and gracing London road. His vision, his ability to read the game and his skill on the ball was a joy to behold as he played in every game during the 1973/74 season.

Players like Freddie will very rarely be seen playing in the lower divisions these days. Astronomical wages mean that players no longer need to drop down the divisions . Freddie joined Posh for £5 more than he was being paid at Manchester City. He was 33 when he joined and was an ex-England international.

Two of his goals, both scored at the Moy's End, are on my list of the best 10 goals I have ever witnessed in my 60 years of following Posh. A volley from some 35-yards vs the Cobblers in 1973 and a free-kick the following season vs Blackburn – top of the Third Division at the time. He also scored the winning goal against Darlington in the final game of our title-winning season.

A memorable player who always appeared to have so much time on the ball and the only player, in my memory, who when he received the ball could make the entire crowd momentarily catch their breath in anticipation of yet another piece of footballing class. He is without doubt in my top team of Posh players of all time.

A quiet but approachable man away from the pitch I was fortunate enough to talk football with him on numerous occasions during his two year stay at Posh. I am proud he was a small but important part of my wonderful memories.

He left Posh at the end of the 1974/75 season due to monetary constraints at the club and joined a Second Division club in Sweden. He later returned to England to take up a management position at Owestry Town.

Brian Seaton

The 73/74 Squad

Forgive me for including an entire squad, especially when we have had a few great teams down the years, but they were the team that made me fall in love with Peterborough United. So they are to blame for a life-long infatuation which, on balance, has bought me more tears than joy and cost me a fortune too.

1973/74 was my first full season of watching Posh as previously I'd been limited to the odd Watney's Cup game and a the limited attention span of a small boy. But I was starting to take football seriously now.

Everything worked out. I only went to home games so I didn't ever see Posh lose. We drew Dirty Leeds at home in the Cup so I got to see the big names and international players.

And the team was set up perfectly. Solid at the back with Chris Turner magnificently solid and I remember, bizarrely, being impressed by Bert Murray's huge thighs. In midfield we were both tenacious and crea-tive. Fred Hill strolling about with all the time in the world to pick a pass and Paul Walker tackling any-thing that moved. Masterful old-fashioned wing-play from Tommy Robson lead to legions of young boys spending hours in the New England practising the Robson penalty winning dive-and-roll.

Up front the stylish John Cozens sported a 'tache that I believe Magnum P.I used as his inspiration while providing the perfect foil to Big Jim.

Some years ago going through boxes of old stuff I found an old Subbuteo companion book which encouraged you to record all your results. it also include a section for you to write down your favourites from the real world of football. Other than Beckenbauer, Cruyff and Neeskens the team was made up entirely of Posh players. World Cup winning Gerd Muller only made the bench.

Love is indeed blind.

Paul Mitchell

David Gregory

1973-1977

Appearances: 148

Goals: 40

David Gregory was my first Posh hero. My first full season of regular attendance had been 73/74 and I loved, still love, the members of that team equally. I was a great admirer of Chris Turner but he was a defender and I was a winger/forward so I needed a role-model I could identify with. One who played in my position but my first choice, Johan Cruyff, had turned down a move to Posh.

The along came Dave. The records tell me he debuted in 73 but he only registered with me in 74/75. He was local - my dad knew his dad or had played against him in Sunday League or at least against someone who knew him and they said he was a good old boy or some such tenuous connection. He had hair that would've have guaranteed him a gig with one of the Glam Rock bands of that era, and he looked a bit like Johan Neeskens – that 1974 Dutch team had a huge effect on me in case you hadn't guessed.

I was nine or ten which was a long time ago but I have an image of him swerving, slaloming past three defenders along the edge of the 18-yard line before twisting his foot around the ball to smash it past the keeper. Those were the sort of goals that I wanted to score.

We moved away from Peterborough in '76 and Dave was one of the players I was looking forward to meeting at the 75th celebration evening. But he declined the invitation to attend as he had a cribbage match that night. Classic Peterborough.

Paul Mitchell

Micky Gynn

1978-1983

Appearances: 177

Goals: 37

Micky Gynn is a bona-fide home-grown Posh hero. Born in Peterborough but raised in Whittlesey, that hotbed of passionate Posh support and Fenland sophistication, he supported Posh as a child. He has also followed the classic old school footballer career trajectory by having a good go at football and then happily getting a proper job, as a postman, once his playing days were over.

Micky was signed by Posh as an U14 before being taken on as an apprentice and he was part of the youth team that got to the quarter-finals of the FA Youth Cup. He signed as a professional in 1978 but Posh were relegated during his first season.

Peter Morris took over as manager and took the bold decision to give some of the younger players a chance in an attempt to galvanise the team. Micky, along with Trevor Quow, Steve Collins and Tony Cliss became regulars. Micky became a regular in midfield and in his final season at Posh scored an incredible

21 goals from midfield. That he achieved this in a distinctly average Posh side already suffering from the debilitating effects of the John Wile makes it even more memorable.

Despite this Micky wasn't offered an improved contract. He then scored twice in a pre-season friendly against Coventry who promptly bid for him. Posh accepted the criminally low bid of £60,000 and he was gone. And who could blame him.

Micky went on to have an excellent career at Coventry culminating in that famous FA Cup win over Tottenham – possibly the only time I've ever wanted Coventry to win a game of football..

David Seaman

1982-1984

Appearances: 106

I started going to London Road in 1983, and as an impressionable 6 year old, my immediate hero was the young, athletic goalkeeper that seemed to never let in a penalty. David Seaman had dropped down from Leeds United to the then lowly 4th Division PUFC in 1982 for just £4,000. He set about repaying that fee and more with some fantastic performances over his two years at London Road, and any idiot could see that he was heading for great things in the game.

However, the big Yorkshireman became the bogey-man of my childhood years! Back in the early 1980's, kids could still wander on the pitch to collect auto-graphs as the teams warmed up. I clambered over the Glebe Road wall and went out to meet Mr Seaman, just as someone took a pot-shot at his goal. I shrieked in 6 year old terror and hit the mud of the London Road End goalmouth. Now fair play to Mr Seaman, he let the ball fly into the net, and quickly bent down to make sure I hadn't been hurt. I was now a bit shocked but despite his kind words of concern his huge, broad Yorkshire voice scared me to death. Now, I am from Stanground so I am used to people talking funny but his voice was instantly inserted into my head as that of a giant monster. For a good few years after I would regularly have nightmares about this 6ft giant with a huge moustache chasing me around a football pitch. Like many of you reading this book, I always had a small sense of pride when Seaman represented England but I could never get that first encounter truly out of my head.

Ray Hankin

1983-1985
Appearances: 36
Goals: 8

I think Ray Hankin was the ultimate cult hero for Posh. I remember he was dropped for apparently misbehaving in some way before an evening match at London Road vs Cobblers. He was supposed to be at the ground anyway, but I saw him sat on a bar stool in the Cock Inn, Werrington the whole night. At the end of the game, the barman told him Posh had won 6-0. Ray remained completely expressionless and ordered another drink.

Paul Leadbitter

Ray played 36 league and League Cup games games for The Posh scoring 8 goals but was sent off in 5 of these games. He made an in instant impact, scoring twice on his debut against Torquay on the10th of September 1983, in a 5-0 win. He joined an elite band of Posh debutants to score twice on their debut as the only other player to achieve this feat was Alan Guy, against Swansea at London Road in March 1979.

Peter Lane, Peterborough United historian had this to say about him: "For a big man Ray possessed such delicate skills on the ball, his trickery a delight to watch and his powerful heading of the ball was second to none. Quickly he became a firm favourite with the Posh fans, but his temper unfortunately got the better of him, hence the five red cards within 18 months. Although I must say I felt a little sorry for him on odd occasions when he was a marked man by some referees."

Greig Shepherd

1984-1987
Appearances: 62
Goals: 10

Many people will say Greig who? as they start reading this, but for a few weeks in 1986 Greig became my hero and a hero to many who were unlucky enough to be following the Posh during the John Wile management years.

Greig came to the Posh having spent four years achieving very little with Norwich City, Eastern Valley (Hong Kong) and Southend United. Signed as a striker for a whopping £8,000 in late 1984 he made his debut away at Exeter City on December 15, 1984 but did nothing in his first few games to indicate the highs to which he'd soon be taking us.

The 1985/6 season started well but the Posh peaked in early September. The league season ended in a scrap against finishing in the bottom four to face the disgrace of applying for re-election, crowds dwindled away and only 1,160 witnessed our home game against Stockport County on April 8. The only ray of sunshine was the FA Cup; after beating Bishops

Stortford in a first round replay we then squeaked past Bath City 1-0 to earn a place in the third round draw. Even thought they were second division at the time, there was much excitement when we were drawn to play Leeds United at home on January 4.

Having started only seven first team games all season, Greig came off the substitutes bench to score with a 67th minute looping header to give the Posh a 1-0 victory. Some will remember the game for John Turner breaking his leg, Scott Sellars being sent off or even the falling snow which covered the pitch by full-time, but I remember this game as Greig's first heroic moment.

The fourth round saw us drawn at home to play Carlisle United who included 24 year-old Mick Halsall in their team. Having been dropped from the starting team the day before, Greig was reprieved when Jackie Gallagher failed a fitness test one hour before the game. On a beautiful sunny day, Greig scored the only goal of the game in the fifth minute when, from a debatable offside position, he hit a low shot past the Carlisle keeper. Greig was a constant threat throughout the game, deserved his Man Of The Match award and was chaired off the pitch by jubilant fans after we held on to make the fifth round.

On a cold February 15, a packed London Road witnessed our fifth round game against Brighton. The pitch was covered with snow and we played with an orange ball for the first time in my memory. In an exciting game, Greig opened the scoring with a 73rd minute header and the Posh nearly won the game thanks to a rather fortunate Errington Kelley snow-assisted strike, but it wasn't to be, and the game finished 2-2.

The replay was postponed a number of times and the Posh finally made the south coast trip on March 3. Greig nearly scored the opening goal but was foiled by Brighton keeper Perry Digweed and the Posh eventually lost 1-0 thanks to a Dean Saunders goal 13 minutes from time, but, were it not for Greig, we would have been visiting Exeter, Swindon and Torquay instead of enjoying our fourth trip to the fifth round of the FA Cup.

Greig played for Posh until 1987 when a knee injury forced him out of the game. He scored 14 goals in 55 games for the Posh but the three cup goals between January and March 1986 made him a legend in my eyes.

Stephen Bull

Errington Kelly

1984-1988
Appearances: 110
Goals: 28

Why Errington? Well, the name alone merits a mention. In December of 1985 I had decided to spend my university holiday – which was my summer in the southern hemisphere for the less well-travelled among you - re-connecting with my roots and spent two months living with my grandparents in Peterborough.

The re-connection was an epic cultural odyssey. That is if your idea of culture is drinking beer, doing the Crown-to-Town, frequenting Millionaires, stumbling out of Canters late on a Sunday night and watching Posh. I hadn't seen Posh play in almost eight years so the masochist in me saw the latter pursuit as quite the treat.

My stay coincided with the beginning of an epic Cup run.. I remember Errington scoring some goals - 21 in 70 appearances between '84-'86 which is positively Mackail-Smith-esque in that team - but mostly I remember his unique wing play. Hoof it and run really fast after it and fall over a lot. Which I think sums up the guile and sophistication of that team perfectly.

Errington helped me re-connect with Posh again. I'm still undecided whether I should be grateful to him or angry with myself that I got dragged back in again.

Paul Mitchell

Gerry McElhinney

1988-1992

Appearances: 111

Goals: 1

Gerry was born in Derry and experienced early sporting success in boxing and Gaelic Football. His Football League career included spells at Bolton, Rochdale and Plymouth. A Plymouth fan's description of "his dive-in head-first style which brought him frequent injuries" elicits a snigger of instant recognition from anyone who saw him play. Plymouth fans probably thought his career was coming to an end when he was given a free transfer at the end of the 1987–8 season. In fact there was life after Home Park and he ran aground at Posh in August 1988, just short of his 32nd birthday, in an inspired transfer swoop by the then management team of Mick Jones and Noel Cantwell. (Remember "Cantwell's Crusade" and Jolly Jack's Bucket Fund?)

Big Mac settled easily into a side boasting three centre backs on a good day and more on a bad one. A suggestion of lack of pace over the first twenty yards was rarely exposed as that season we played a sweeper system which allowed Gary "Archie" Andrews hours of practice behind the back four, perfecting his fifty yard ball up field. It was only when he played a couple of games in midfield that we realised that this was the only ball he could play; still it exercised the YTS lads retrieving balls from behind the Moy's End stand throughout the game. Fans' loud and frequent complaints that this system was too defensive particularly in homes games, were countered by the boss's persuasive argument of the need to keep a clean sheet at all costs although our subsequent final league placing of 17th in Division 4 with 74 goals conceded suggests this was not a total success. Mac did not attract much attention from the normally vituperative crowd, their vitriol being chiefly reserved for the hapless Keith Oakes, at whom they brayed continually.

Close season and Big Gerry was the surprise announcement as Youth Team manager and it seemed clear that his playing days were numbered, particularly as we had signed Dave Robinson, an apparently talented centre half from Halifax for £100,000.

But ... after 12 games an injury to Keith Oakes saw our man recalled as an emergency replacement and there he remained until the end of the season. Initially regarded more or less as a good, honest trier, over the course of season the crowd took Big Mac to their hearts and elevated him to folk hero status. He was Supporters' Player of the Year and Directors' Player of the Year, with a special citation for" levels of enthusiasm, determination and commitment".

He visibly grew in stature with the crowd's adoration, initially tongue-in-cheek but ultimately ungrudgingly wholehearted. He still had the stooped run of an 80 year old, he still looked knackered before a ball had been kicked, but now the hoof over the stand had been replaced by the mazy dribble out of defence. This was all distilled into one near end-of-season game when we actually played well.

In the first half he went up for a ball with our Mark Hine, who rather unsportingly landed on Mac's leg. After a few minutes treatment he resumed with, we assumed, nothing worse than a broken leg. Sure enough he was out again after half-time none the worse for it.

Midway through the second half he went down again after a clash of heads - he hadn't spilt blood for a couple of weeks so this looked promising. What got up defied description, even for Big Mac. The head was still the same shape but was presumably lacerated from ear to ear as he appeared to be leaking blood from all points. Even with the constant use of the sponge for the rest of the game the flow could not be adequately staunched and there were shouts urging him to stay away from the touchline and get back to the middle of the park where he wouldn't frighten the women and children.

Naturally, an injury which would have hospitalised a heavyweight boxer did not adversely affect Mac's game until, right at the end, came the coup de gras. In the last minute he embarked on a meandering dribble from his penalty area that would have made Beckenbauer look pedestrian. A perfect lay-off was naturally not taken advantage of by our forwards and an opponent soon lumped a high ball over our back four. As Big Mac chased it back towards the corner he didn't nod it into touch, he didn't launch it over the stand – he flicked it up and stood by the corner flag bouncing it up and down on his head a la George Best until, overawed, the ref blew for time several seconds later. As the crowd roared its salute Mac allowed himself a dab with the sponge and a quick raise of the eyebrows in recognition. Poetry! Oh, and the Youth Team? Well, they finished bottom of the Purity Youth League with 2 wins, 22 defeats and conceded 82 goals.

Phil Harburn

Oooooh, Gerry, Gerry

I didn't find out until many years later that big Gerry had been a highly successful Gaelic football player before he took up football professionally, but looking back now it makes perfect sense. The genial Irishman's life story would no doubt make an interesting read, as he was also a junior Ulster boxing champion, played football in the USA in the late 1970's and was part of the Northern Ireland team that won the last ever British Home Championship. Gerry arrived at London Road in the twilight of his career, in a cut-price £10,000 move from Plymouth Argyle, where the fans affectionately nicknamed him "Rambo".

I have never witnessed a player able to kick a football so high and so far as Gerry. During his 3 years at London Road (1988-1991), I don't recall him passing the ball once, which was probably for the best with the standard of players around him. If the ball came anywhere near him, as he swung his tree trunk legs the shout from the stands would go up "Hooooooooof" and Gerry would launch that ball down the pitch even if stood in 10 yards of space. Along with Mick Halsall, Gerry would give his all for the Posh teams that he played in, if that meant sticking his head in amongst the boots to clear the ball then so be it. Gerry, and the evergreen Keith Oakes may have been amongst the slowest centre half pairings that the club have ever put out, but no opposition centre forward ever finished the game without a few bruises and the occasional bandaged head.

The London Road crowd had a great relationship with Gerry, with the familiar "Oooooh, Gerry, Gerry" regularly ringing out before kick-off. Gerry battled gamely against injuries during his time at London Road, with his dedication and will to win rewarded with a coaching role under the management of Chris Turner.

Oooh Gerry Gerry! I always remember a league cup tie away at QPR when they were topflight and we were division 4. Their forward lobbed our keeper, the ball bounced on about the 6 yard line, and was just about to go in when Gerry appeared from nowhere, and performed a completely out of character athletic overhead clearance.

Goodness knows how many years ago that was now, but it's something that I shall never forget. Much like losing my virginity, only Gerry wasn't there at the time.

Lincoln Posh

George Berry

1990-1991
Appearances: 30
Goals: 7

As a 13 year old I used to stand on the Glebe, right near the front, and 'Denzil', playing at right back, used to constantly chat to the crowd during the game - can you imagine any player doing that now? On one occasion during the 90/91 promotion season I remember him getting down the wing and attempting an ambitious first time cross into the box. He messed it up completely and just sliced it down the touchline. Fortunately, the ball just stopped dead, spinning on the touchline but staying in play and Noel Luke or someone got there ahead of their left back. Denzil turned round to us after getting some stick and said "Eh! That was a precision ball that was!"

I remember a friendly was arranged at the end of that season to celebrate winning promotion – achieved courtesy of the ball skimming of George's afro and trickling into the net - and the crowd all ran on the pitch at the end to congratulate the players. I was getting a few of the players to autograph my programme. I ran up to Denzil and said "bet you can't wait for next season eh Denzil?" He just signed my programme and said "not me son, I'll be on the dole next week". I was gutted for him.

A real character in the true sense of the word, not the Barry Fry sense.

Richard Clay

Noel Luke

1986-1993
Appearances: 337
Goals: 31

Noel "Doris" Luke was a very average right winger when he arrived at London Road in 1986, following spells with WBA and Mansfield. John Wile did not achieve much during his time in the London Road hot seat, aside from the 1985/86 FA Cup run, but he did convert Noel into a highly effective right back. His marauding overlapping runs and his obvious love for the club were key features of his 277 appearances for PUFC over a 7 year period. Noel dug in and helped the club through the grim days of the mid-to-late 1980's, and was a trusted lieutenant of the swash-buckling midfield general that was Mick Halsall.

In the 1988/89 season, Worrell Sterling arrived at London Road from Watford and he and Noel became firm friends on and off the pitch. Like an earlier, and more handsome, version of David Beckham and Gary Neville... their right sided combination play would go on to be a key feature of both the 1990/91 and 1991/92 promotion seasons. The fact that Noel only ever seemed to pass to Worrell was not missed by the crowd, especially the kids where we stood in the Glebe who would regularly sing "Noel passed to Worrell, so Worrell passed it back".

After leaving Posh, Noel went onto to brief spells with Rochdale and Boston before making a welcome return to London Road to manage the much missed "Posh Pub".

Why the Doris nickname? It was the name of a character in Crossroads. Probably best to ask your Dad, no actually better ask your Grandad.

Here is what Noel had to say when I caught up with him recently:

Whats your best ever Posh moment?

"That's easy, getting promoted at Wembley."

What's your worst Posh moment?

"Getting released the day before transfer deadline way back when."

What was it like playing under Chris Turner?

"Playing for Chris was very rewarding in many ways as he was a big character and an excellent defensive coach. His first ever team talk went along the lines of 'I'm the King of the Jungle and anyone that doesn't like it they can f**k off now'.so that was his style of management."

Now its nearly 20 years ago, can you tell us any secrets surrounding the 2 promotion season?

"On the way back from Wembley there was a crate of Champagne stowed underneath the team bus. The manager decreed that we were not allowed to have it as he reckoned we'd all be drunk prior to our reception at the Marriot Hotel. In hindsight he was probably right but what a meanie."

Was it written into your contract that you and Worrell had to pass to each other a certain number of times in every match?

"That was just telepathy from one room-mate to another."

Mick Halsall

1987-1993
Appearances: 315
Goals: 38

Every fan on the London Road terraces wanted to see a little bit of themselves in 'Scouse'. In terms of passion, commitment and a desire for PUFC to win matches I don't think Mick will ever be beaten.

He arrived at London Road in a particularly grim period of the clubs history with no money available, his £25,000 transfer fee was paid for through fans donations to 'Cantwell's Crusade'. We had watched carthorses and journeymen plod around the pitch for years, leading the club almost inevitably to the bottom of Division Four. Mick played a huge part in changing all that. He came into the team and stamped his authority all over it within about 10 minutes of his debut. He was the on-field captain that every manager dreamed of. He never gave up, he never let his team give up and though this is sometimes forgotten, he could play a bit as well.

Mick was a player that the crowd, and by all accounts his fellow players, could relate to. The London

Road End had an almost ritual song for Mick, with them singing There's Only One Scouse Bastard which Mick would ignore, before the chant of There's Only One Micky Halsall would break out and he would turn, flash that wide gap-toothed smile and applaud.

Every Posh fan of that era will have their favourite memory of Mick, whether it be his crazy celebration of the winner at Huddersfield, his bust-up with Wayne Biggins or him lifting the play-off trophy on that boiling hot Wembley day. My favourite moment would when in the home leg of the 1991/92 play off. They were 2-1 up with the clock ticking down, and it really felt like our chances of getting to Wembley were gone. So, who better to turn to at such at time then Mick? He picked up the ball on the right hand side of the area, powered forward and smashed it into the top corner. The whole ground erupted as he ran around swirling his arms in celebration. We were back in the tie and ultimately set on the path to Wembley.

I was lucky enough to sit next to Mick at the 75th birthday celebration event, and he remains an avid Posh fan. He didn't want to reminisce about the good old days; he wanted to know if CMS could fire the goals to get us promoted.

Worrell Sterling

Appearances: 233
Goals:38

Perhaps the greatest compliment that Worrell Sterling was paid by the Posh supporters during his time at London Road is that he was given the same chant as the legendary Tommy Robson *"We've Got Worrell, Worrell, Worrell Sterling On The Wing"*. The hard working yet skilful right winger arrived in Peterborough late in the 1988/89 season for a then club record fee of £70,000.

Sterling would have to work through the hugely disappointing 1989/90 season with the club before Chris Turner rolled back into the stadium and launched the club on the road to promotion. Sterling almost instantly struck up an on-field relationship with Noel Luke down the Posh right, and his expert crosses and the occasional goal were always vital to the cause.

Sterling was key in both the 1990/91 and 1991/92 promotions. In many ways he is the forgotten man of that momentous night when Posh beat Huddersfield in the Play-Off Semi Final 2nd Leg. As detailed elsewhere in this book, Steve Cooper was the hero of that night with a stunning diving header. However, if it hadn't been for the pace, anticipation and immense bravery of Worrell Sterling to score the equaliser that night, the whole fairytale may never have come true.

Sterling left Posh in 1993 to join Bristol Rovers, but still lives locally and lectures in Sports Science at Huntingdon Regional College.

Dave Robinson

1989-1993
Appearances: 123
Goals: 10

'Big Dave Robbo' came to London Road from Halifax for a club record £100,000 in the summer of 1989. Despite his on-going injury problems, he went on to produce 123 performances in a Posh shirt that bristled with power, aggression and an unflinching will to win.

Robbo quickly settled into life at glamorous London Road, well compared to Halifax Towns old ground, The Shay, it was like moving to Monte Carlo. Posh had been served up some pretty grim central defenders in the mid to late 1980's, Wakeley Gage springs to mind, but Robbo was the real deal. He was amazingly quick for a big man, with his long rake-like legs carrying him over the London Road mud at great speed. He could play a bit, but would usually prefer to just do the simple "agricultural" thing whenever the ball came to him. Injury put paid to most of his participation in the 1990/91 promotion season, but he did come back into the team for the run-in. He was then a huge part of the success that followed in the "Wembley" season of 1991/92.

Much is, quite rightly, made of the team spirit amongst the current Posh squad, but back in 1991/92 , something very special was brewing in the depths of the London Road dressing room. Led by Mick Halsall with the likes of Robbo, Lukey and King Kenny as his trusted lieutenants, this side never gave up and fought and scrapped their way to that glorious Wembley afternoon.

I bumped into Robbo in a City Centre pub many years after that afternoon, and after he graciously accepted a pint, he happily talked about that "special time" and that Chris Turner was "by far the best manager, I ever had. He understood what it meant to be a centre half, and just told me to go out and be horrible, do whatever it took to stop the bastards scoring past us."

Unfortunately Robbo's injury record remained poor and it was a shock that despite his brilliant form, Chris Turner used all his guile to persuade Notts County to spend £400,000 on Robbo's battered knees (they got the rest of him as well for that price!). Robbo made only a handful of appearances for Notts County before retiring on March 24th 1994.

Garry Kimble

1991-1992

Appearances: 44

Goals: 6

Some players are in this book for season upon season of exemplary service to PUFC, others are in here on the basis of one moment of magic. Garry Kimble is the epitome of that second category. Kimble only played one season for Posh as a two paced (forwards and backwards) winger who didn't have the football brain to beat players or play many decent passes. However, on a very special night in PUFC history – 3.12.1991 - Kimble managed to do something very special, he scored the winning goal in the League Cup tie with Liverpool.

Just to put that into context, the League Cup then was a competition that the big teams took seriously. Liverpool were in Europe that season and had only just begun their long wait for another league title. They had the likes of Molby, Saunders, McManaman and of course Bruce Grobelaar in their side.

A sold out London Road of 14,114 didn't really believe Posh could get anything from the game but were determined to make an incredible noise to roar the team on.

In the 19th minute, a Worrell Sterling cross was seen by Grobelaar who came charging out his goal to make the catch. Instead of making the catch the madcap keeper sent the ball spinning out to Garry Kimble who steadied himself and knocked the ball into an empty net. The old place went crazy, with a noise that I did not witness again until the home leg of the play-off's V MK Dons in 2011. At the final whistle, with a 1-0 win secured, fans flooded onto the pitch to lift the players to the tunnel. Kimble found himself all over the next day's national newspapers, with t-shirts being printed by Hereward Sports featuring his smiling face.

The story does not end brilliantly for Mr Kimble though, in terms of PUFC. The iron-willed Chris Turner saw him as a weak link in the side and when Bobby Barnes came in from Northampton in the January of 1992, Kimble's career at London Road was effectively over. He left that summer to play at Dagenham, but thanks to that one moment will live on as a Posh legend.

Marcus Ebdon

1991-1997
Appearances: 173
Goals: 16

When Marcus Ebdon joined Posh in the summer of 1991, he could not have imagined the place in the folklore of the club that he would occupy just a few months later. Marcus Ebdon provided possibly the best pass in the history of Peterborough United on that boiling hot afternoon of 24th May 1992.

Ebdon was a cultured midfielder with Welsh Under 21 caps, who spent the early months of that season alongside Mick Halsall in the midfield engine room. As the season wore on, Chris Turner used the maverick skills of Gary Cooper alongside Scouse and Ebdon took a back seat. The easily combustible Cooper - think Joey Barton but ginger - went missing one week, and I don't mean on the pitch during a game, I mean literally went missing, and Ebdon returned to the starting line up.

During the game at Wembley, Ebdon went about his work in his usual silky, cultured manner. His footballing education at Everton ensured that even in the rabid world of Division 3, he refused to panic when on the ball. His magical moment came in the dying seconds of the game, when he nudged the ball into space deep in his own half, looked up and saw Kenny Charley getting his knackered legs moving for one last run. Ebdon then flights a beautiful pass into the on-rushing Kenny's path and the rest is history.

Ebdon continued to grace the Posh midfield until 1997, with the 1995/96 season of particular note, as the normally mild mannered midfielder managed to get himself sent off twice that season.

Ken Charlery

1991-1993, 1994-1995, 1996-1997
Appearances: 216
Goals: 80

Nothing will ever quite match the moment at Wembley 1992 when "King" Kenny Charlery scored the 89th minute winner to send Posh up to the old League 1. However, there is a cracking piece of audio commentary knocking around from BBC Radio Cambs where the commentator screeches "He's in with a chance, he's into the area.....HE'S DONE IT, Ken Charlery, 89 minutes". Just writing that, sends a shiver down the spine.

Ken Charlery ended the 1991/92 season as a true Posh hero but he started it out of the team, and with many fans wondering why Chris Turner had paid brought him in from Maidstone the previous season. Indeed, during the 4-0 thumping we received at WBA in September 1991 the home fans openly laughed when Charlery skied a sitter over the top of the stand. As always, we really should have trusted in the judgement of Chris Turner.

Charlery didn't get his first goal that season until he scored in the 1-1 draw with Reading at London Road on 19th October. The goal that day, seemed to spark something inside Ken's head and he went on a brilliant run that really did see him turn from zero to hero in scoring 26 goals in all competitions that season.

Charlery even managed to get himself the nickname of "King Kenny" following his 2 goals at Wembley in 1992. Kenny was as busy off the pitch as he was on it during his time at London Road. Aside from the much publicised fight with Mick Bodley, our lawyers will not allow us to make further comment.

I remember being on the pitch at Leeds Road after that famous play-off semi win and managing to shake Kenny by the hand. The great man appeared distracted, and whilst the players and the thousands of Posh fans danced around that pitch, Kenny had spotted young lady he like the look of in the crowd and went off to chat her up!

We should never underestimate - and Kenny himself certainly didn't - the financial boost that his transfers gave to the football club. Kenny left Posh in the 1992/93 season to sign for Watford but returned to London Road the following year. He was voted

PUFC player of the year for the 2nd time in 1994/95. A certain Mr B Fry took him to Birmingham in 1995 but he returned for a third spell with Posh in 1996. In truth, he endured a pretty torrid time at London Road in this spell, and was not helped by being part of a dire Posh side. He left PUFC for the third and final time (as a player) in 1997.

Tony Adcock

1991-1994
Appearances: 123
Goals: 39

Tony Adcock was already a legendary figure at Colchester United, before a double spell at the old County Ground saw him become the same at Northampton Town. In his spells at the Cobblers, Adcock scored an impressive 40 goals in 107 appearances. Normally, I wouldn't bother writing about player's goals/games at our local rivals but those excellent stats made his signature for Posh even sweeter. Chris Turner enhanced his God-like status amongst the London Road faithful by taking advantage of the Cobblers financial crisis in January 1992 and signing Adcock and the wing wizard that was Bobby Barnes for just £25,000.

Turner had seen that the team had half-a-chance of promotion that season and the two ex-Cobblers added that slice of skill and experience that the team needed. In his first full appearance, Adcock scored twice as Posh hammered Fulham 4-1 (those were the days). What was key for me that day was his class, his awareness and the fact that he always seemed to have so much time on the ball when taking a shot at goal. He instantly became my favourite Posh player. All in all, he got seven league goals that season, despite a long barren run. He formed an excellent partnership with Kenny Charlery, which regularly terrorised defences in the old Division 3. Adcock was also the man trying desperately to head in Charlery's shot for the first Posh goal at Wembley. Many years later, I asked Tony about that 'goal' and he insists it was over the line and that he was only trying to head it so that he could "claim the goal, as I hadn't scored for weeks".

In the 1992/93 season he took on the goal scoring responsibilities, after Charlerys departure to Watford and played a huge part in the clubs best ever football league finish that season. For me, the greatest ever Adcock moment arrived that season, on a freezing cold March night at (at the time) our fierce local rivals, Cambridge United. Posh were 2-0 down at half-time and looked totally out of it before big John McGlashan got away with kicking their keeper in the face, knocked it to Adcock who prodded the ball home. With ten minutes to go, Adcock managed to get a slight touch on a free kick that flew into the net and it was 2-2. His wild celebration, in front of the massed ranks of the Posh fans will live with me for a long time.

Bobby Barnes

Appearances: 49
Goals: 9

Bobby Barnes may only have played 49 times for The Posh, but my memory tells me that every one of those appearances featured a trick, a piece of skill or a pass that has the fans purring. Barnes was not the classic old-fashioned winger but was always looking to take players on and have a shot at goal.

Barnes was stolen away from Northampton along with Tony Adcock in January 1992, and like Adcock went on to have an exceptional impact on the PUFC season. For many years, even after they had left the club, Posh fans took great delight in singing "Thank You Very Much for Tony and Bobby" to their Cobblers counterparts.

Barnes played a key role in two of the biggest goals in the clubs history in the space of just a couple of weeks in 1992. After playing exceedingly well at Huddersfield in the Play Off Semi-Final 2nd Leg, a clearly knackered Barnes shuttled down the right flank and sent over the perfect cross for Steve Cooper to write himself into Posh folklore. Barnes made his mark on the final against Stockport by sending over a peach of a corner which Charlery headed against the underside of the bar and over/onto the line, depending on which team you supported that day.

Barnes left London Road in 1994 having become a peripheral figure and moved to Partick Thistle. After retiring in 1996, he joined the PFA staff and has made a great success of his career and is currently Chief Executive of the PFA.

Steve Cooper

1992

Appearances: 2

Goals: 1

On page 119 of Andy Groom and Mick Robinson's The Official History of Peterborough United Football Club there is a photograph.

It's a photograph that means so much to any true Posh supporter, an image unlike any other – unique. It's a dark Thursday night, the 14 May 1992. It's the second leg of the Third Division Play-Off Semi-Final and the scores are level. It's six minutes from the end of normal time - not that anything about this game has been normal.

In the picture four Huddersfield defenders stand rooted to the spot. Tony Adcock stands, mouth half open in anticipation. And in the foreground there he is, not standing, not running but airborne, both feet off the ground, eyes firmly planted on the ball that he's just sent flying towards and into the goal. The man with the golden header. The header of the golden ball. The goal that proved to be golden. The goal that sent Posh to Wembley.

Anyone who sees that photograph never forgets it. Anyone who remembers that goal knows exactly what it meant. Anyone who knows anything about Posh always thanks the man who scored it.

Steve Cooper, Super Cooper, The man who unlocked the Wembley door.

People like me live for moments like that. People like me remember and celebrate. A photograph like that; a goal like that; a memory like that; a man like that.

Paul Donnelly

Lee Howarth

1991-1994
Appearances: 69
Goals: 1

Lee didn't play that many games for Posh and failed to establish himself as a regular member of the first team during his three years at London Road. He does however; fully merit a place in this book due to a moment of defensive wizardry at Wembley in 1992.

Howarth's moment is often overlooked when people reminisce about Wembley '92, mainly because so much else happened during that 90 mins, from disputed Posh goals, to disallowed Stockport goals and then of course the winner in the last minute. However, in all likelihood if it had not been for Lee Howarth, Stockport would have been promoted that day and not the Posh.

Less than a minute after Stockport had equalised, with their blood sensing victory, the human beanpole that is Kevin Francis headed the ball towards the Posh goal. With Fred Barber beaten, the Posh hordes at the other end of the ground feared the worst, but then Howarth popped into view. Lee was not a small lad, and could hardly be described as athletic but he contorted his frame up into the air and performed a textbook volley off the line. Francis stood open mouthed in disbelief that he had been denied the winning goal.

Minutes later it was "Ebdon to Charlery" and we all went home deliriously happy.

Marc 'Ginge' Tracy

I have many fond memories of my time at Posh and it's hard to say which is best but if pushed I'd probably that the night at Leeds Road, Huddersfield in the 1992 play-offs was a special night. Probably better than Wembley in a strange way - Posh fans there that night would know what I mean.

My worst memory was probably the day I left Posh - It hurt to be told by a certain person that I was being made redundant and I was no longer wanted.

Any secrets to reveal? Well, I saw and heard many things during my time and they will stay with me - what I will share is that the team once left me behind by accident in Newcastle after we stopped off after the game so I hitch-hiked back to St James Park then caught the train home and arrived back waiting for them at London Road. I was only 15 - I was never late for the coach again.

Being at Posh was an amazing experience where I made many friends and learned so many important aspects which have helped me in subsequent roles. Posh will always hold great memories for me. The 1992 season in particular was an amazing season with many great memories capped with a fantastic victory at Wembley. Being in a winning squad photo at Wembley is what every youngster dreams of so I know how lucky I am and thankful to that squad and management during that time.

Chris Turner is a special person who gave me my opportunity and who I hold in high regard and respect. I felt my relationship with Posh fans was good and the friendly and abusive banter I received by them was fun as I warmed up many Posh goalkeepers. Great memories and I could go and on about my time at Posh.

Ginge

Dominic Iorfa

1992-1994
Appearances: 32
Goals: 10

How can I describe Dominic Iorfa? Well, an old school Shaun Batt with less skill and control would be a start. He played for Posh between 1992-1994 and became a cult hero for his eccentric and inconsistent displays in the second and third tier.

Iorfa will forever live in the hearts of many a Posh fan for his barnstorming demolition of Viv Anderson v Barnsley, who consequently tabled a £350K bid the next day to try and sign him - it was refused, his cheeky goal in a 5-2 victory against Sunderland and an absolute screamer away to Oxford.

Interspersed with his magnificent goals and performances was absolute garbage. At times it was hard to believe he was actually a footballer the way he mis-controlled the ball, his failure to pass to a team mate and his inability to head a ball - I think he was scared. Despite this, Iorfa is a name that most Posh fans will remember forever and you'll still occasionally hear a chant of his name at matches.

Even as he departed our club his comic timing didn't fail him. His reasoning for leaving Posh was because 'it was too cold', however Iorfa soon signed for Falkirk - I think he got Falkirk mixed up with Faliraki and thought he was off to the Mediterranean instead of central Scotland. And that sums up what Dominic Iorfa perfectly.

Neil Bates

If you'd asked me in 1992 which team I supported, I'd likely have said West Ham, having been taken there a few times by a family friend. But, newly enriched by the vast sums I was being paid by the Evening Telegraph as a paperboy, I decided to pay my gate money at London Road and accompany my mates Burton, Wilson and Buckingham to see Posh versus Sunderland. They were as big a club then as they are now and had been FA Cup finalists the previous season. Posh were well up for the game, riding on the success of their promotion to the old First Division and were already well in command by the time Nigerian striker Dominic Iorfa came on for Tony Philliskirk in the 75th minute, but it was his goal that proved the most memorable. After a neat through ball from Tony Adcock, Iorfa raced clear and metby the keeper he veered away and seemed to be heading home for his dinner. Then suddenly he turned and launched a sublime chip over the keeper for Posh's fifth. That was it for me, we went crazy, I was hooked and big Dom was my new hero.

For me, Dominic Iorfa is the epitome of a cult hero. His career may suggest he was not prodigiously talented, although Trevor Francis once parted with £145,000 of someone else's money to take him from Belgium to QPR - a decision seemingly based on Iorfa's international record - but his performances at several of his clubs made him a firm favourite on the terraces. His main attribute was his blistering pace. Sometimes he even took the ball with him.

In his first season at Posh he was largely utilized as a super sub. I remember the excitement when he came on against Spurs in the 1-1 draw at London Road in the FA Cup in 94, by then the chants of "Iorfa-Iorfa" were well established, as he tore down the wing and scared the life out of the Spurs defence. But Dom's legendary status had long since been secured, on that cold November afternoon the season before. His strike against Sunderland was not the only special goal he scored for Posh. Most fans remember a 30-yard stunner against Oxford in one of his last games for club.

Peterborough is a small city, so maybe I shouldn't have been too surprised when I mentioned to a family friend that I was going to write a piece on Dominic Iorfa and he announced that he knew him. Turns out that Enzo Cozzetto's wife Antonietta worked at Thomas Cook, who used to prefer to sponsor their local club. Opposite her desk was a big poster of the Posh Squad. When they encountered the lonely figure of Dominic Iorfa sat in the Newark Hotel it was Antonietta that recognised the new Posh player and suggested to Enzo that he should go and have a chat. Iorfa was not only delighted at being recognised, but also, being Peterborough, that someone had actually spoken to him. For the time Iorfa was at Posh, the Cozzetto's were Dom's link to the Peterborough public, they even went to each others houses for dinner. When his family arrived Dom moved to Whittlesey and Enzo got free tickets for home games.

Following appearances for Southend, Falkirk, a stint in China, Ireland and the Conference, Dominic Iorfa made his way back to Nigeria where he is currently chairman of Premier League outfit Lobi Stars. Tim

Knighton, official stalker for Posh fanzine Blue Moon, once unsuccessfully attempted to arrange a meeting with him in London, although a problematic telephone call to Nigeria at least revealed Big Dom was still tracking Posh's results. Similar attempts to reach him for this piece - via his son, currently a defender in the Wolves academy - were also unsuccessful and thus Big Dom continues to avoid his pursuers.

Big Dom's goal versus Sunderland remains one my favourite Posh moments. His performances may have been erratic and his ability to go from woeful to wonderful in moments both exciting and frustrating, but that is what made him a true Posh cult hero.

Steven Turner

David Farrell

1997-2006
Appearances: 313
Goals: 53

David Farrell was born in Castle Bromwich, Birmingham, on 11th November 1971 and there is some significance to this date as David was born under the astrological star sign of Scorpio. Quite fitting when consideration is given to the amount of defenders who have been first tormented, then stung by his poise and pace, and finally despatched by the fleet-footed wide man.

David's first club of note was Redditch United, but after just seven games he caught the attention of Aston Villa manager Ron Atkinson who signed David for the bargain price of £45,000 in January 1992. Quite remarkably, David duly made his Premiership debut a few months later from the substitutes' bench, replacing Dwight Yorke as Villa pounded out a draw at Oldham.

In a Villa Park career of over two and a half years, David made a handful of further appearances before moving to ambitious Wycombe Wanderers for

£100,000 and subsequently made over seventy appearances for the Chairboys, delivering a quality of service that made Miguel de Souza appear to be an attractive target (for at least one gavel-wielding team boss).

Before the start of the 97-98 season, David had followed his old chum De Souza to London Road. This proved to be one of the most astute signings made by Barry Fry although David's free transfer may not have indicated this at the time.

Posh started the 97-98 season in style, overcoming an opening day defeat to string together some respectable results. The League Cup first round tie at Fratton Park produced a minor shock as Posh beat Portsmouth 2-1 with Faz opening his Posh account.

David had become a notable player at London Road, always eager to take on defenders and never wasting an opportunity to deliver the coup de gras himself should the Posh front line prove unable to arrive at the scene of the incident with the same rapidity as the flying winger. His incessant tormenting of punch-drunk defenders was arguably making him one of the most cynically fouled players ever to represent Posh. Notwithstanding the hefty challenges, it also became evident that marking Faz completely out of the game was like trying to nail a blancmange to a passing Formula One car.

Faz's golden moment at Posh was in the 2nd leg of the play-off semi final against Barnet. It was to be one of those special occasions when a match delivers everything it could possibly promise and much, much more.

Few games bear the hallmark of an individual player whose contribution is so magnificent that the match itself becomes synonymous with the name of that player. Instances include the Matthews Cup-Final in 1953 when the future Sir Stanley repeatedly tore the Bolton Wanderers defence to shreds though somehow contrived not to score himself. On 17 May 2000, Posh commenced what was to indisputably become the Faz Play-Off Semi-final!

The hat-trick Faz scored that day will live on in the memory of every posh fan, it is without doubt the greatest hat trick of all time, let alone at London Road.

Posh went on to win promotion at Wembley with Andy Clarke scoring the only goal in a 1-0 win against Darlington

David Farrell had won the hearts of the Posh faithful within a few weeks of arriving and it was an enduring love-affair. In the days of unscrupulous football agents and the Bosman ruling, loyalty has proved to be a rare commodity but together with fellow fans' favourite, Mark Tyler, Faz has proved to be a wonderful servant to the club.

It is also worth noting that it takes a very special player indeed to hold the often fickle attention of Barry Fry for nearly a decade. The skill and commitment of David Farrell has both put bums on seats and regularly lifted the same bums out of those seats when in possession of the ball during Posh offensives.

Always sublime, regularly exciting and, on certain occasions, capable of true world-class genius. Like the Scorpion Tattoo on Faz's left shoulder, the image of Faz destroying his opponents is likewise indelibly etched in the hearts and minds of his adoring fans at London Road.

This article was first published in the fanzine Blue Moon

Mark Tyler

1993-2009

Appearances: 490

"Tyler, Tyler, Tyler" was the chant that greeted Mark Tyler on the 485 times that he represented PUFC*. The mixture of brilliant shot stopping, dedication to the club and calm approach led to Tyler becoming a firm favourite. Like many others featured in this book, Tyler had the misfortune of playing with some of the worst players that ever graced the blue and white shirt. However, he didn't moan he just got on with his work and enjoyed the glory days, such as Wembley 2000, when they came along.

He was a lovely bloke off the pitch, who was always happy to give his time to local community causes, and promote the good name of Peterborough United. On the pitch, only his height prevented him for adding to his solitary England U21 cap, and moving up the leagues with a move away from London Road. Whenever talk of PUFC's greatest ever keeper crops up on the internet forums, Tyler always gets his fair share of the votes.

Tyler came over from Norwich as a young lad, when Kit Carson took over the Youth system at London Road. He made his debut as a 17 year old, in a 4-0 thumping away at Birmingham in 1994, and then went out on loan the following season. From the start of the 1997-98 season, Tyler made the No.1 jersey his own and it would stay that way until Joe Lewis arrived and displaced him in 2007. After a variety of loan moves, he made the permanent switch to Luton Town in June 2009, where he remains at their first choice keeper.

* Ok, I grant ya, it may not have been sung for the first few games he played! Pedants

Andy Clarke

1999-2005
Appearances: 199
Goals: 71

Andy 'The Cake' Clarke will be fondly remembered by Posh fans for a variety of reasons, not least of which is the winner in the 1999/2000 Play-Off Final. On that rain lashed night, Posh were not playing well when Clarke managed the squeeze the ball home and send the fans home happy, if a little soggy. Clarke had only arrived at London Road the previous summer after eight years at Wimbledon FC. That goal afforded him legendary status and he went on to score 57 in total for Posh in 230 appearances over a 6 year period. I am the only one who is amazed that he made as many as appearances as that for the club?

Clarke had blistering pace and used it to great effect on many occasions but he also had a very poor "footballing brain". His ability to stray offside, even in situations where it was far easier to remain onside, provoked much muttering and laughter amongst the fans.

His other iconic moment occurred during a game against Brentford. In a rare Posh goal-fest Clarkey rounded the keeper, took the ball to a yard from the net and then got down on all fours to nod the ball home. Apparently hugely disrespectful to the Brentford team, their fans, and their families but very, very funny for us Posh fans.

After a game against local rivals Cambridge United - remember them? - in December 2001, Clarke failed a random drug test. In March of the following year, the FA banned Clarke for just 4 weeks, seemingly recognising his defence that he had simply "eaten some cake that someone had given him". That is a defence that would now surely lead to at least a six month ban.

The 37 year old Clarke finally left London Road in 2005 and went on to run a market stall back in his home borough of Barnet.

Kit Carson

1993-2001

Tyler, Davies, Etherington, Drury are just four of the PUFC players that owe a huge debt of gratitude to Kit Carson for their successful footballing careers. Never before, or since, have the London Road faithful taken a Youth Team Manager to their hearts like they did with Kit.

Kit came to London Road from Norwich City in 1993, bringing with him a wealth of young talent. Many of the players that Kit helped on the road to success went on to have brilliant careers at London Road, and indeed went on to earn the club significant sums in transfer fees. Kit was given the time, space and resource to build a youth set-up from grass-roots level and obtain the prestigious Academy Licence. His greatest on the field achievement was the run to the Semi-Final of the FA Youth Cup in 1997-98. Of that team, an amazing 10 players were given professional contracts at London Road.

Kit left London Road in 2001, after an on-going public row with Mr Fry - a rift now healed judging by the warm way they greeted each other st the 75th

Celebrations - and with the clubs Academy being downgraded to a Centre of Excellence to cut costs. Despite his departure Kit retains a deep affection for the club and in particular the fans.

Indeed the list of players that he has worked with over the years is quite stunning and includes the Posh players mentioned above as well as the likes of Craig Bellamy, Jack Collison and Danny Mills.

Adam Drury

1993-2001
Appearances: 165
Goals: 2

From the moment Adam Drury stepped onto the field in a Peterborough United shirt, he exuded a calm, thoughtful, athletic air of left-back authority.

It was unfortunate for Adam that he broke into the first team at London Road during the Dark Ages of the mid-1990's when the team was being chopped and changed and usually ridiculed all around him.

Drury maintained his own high standards throughout his time at London Road, and unlike other players of the era, only did his talking out on the pitch.

He could defend like a lion when he needed to, or offer an excellent overlapping full back option when the opportunity arose. He was part of the play-off winning side in 2000 but by then had seen his good friends Davies and Etherington (as well as the less successful McEever and Billington) leave London Road for the bright lights of the top of the football pyramid.

He finally left London Road to join Norwich City in 2001, where he remains to this day.

Dean Hooper

1995, 1999-2002
Appearances: 121
Goals: 2

July 1999: Matthew Etherington and Simon Davies had just spent a week at Old Trafford, training with Manchester United, allowing Alex Ferguson to get a closer look at this pair of Posh Academy products. A 17-year-old former Deacon's School pupil and a 19-year-old Welshman were on the brink of greatness. A move to Manchester United would be the biggest transfer deal in Peterborough United history and as a cub reporter on the local rag, I wanted in on the action. I was to visit the training ground at Castor, where I would nab young Mushy and Digger. We would instantly hit it off and head into town for a few beers – they'd be Gazza to my Chris Evans and Danny Baker. I could ride their coat-tails all the way to the Premier League – celebrity nightclubs, a private box at Old Trafford – I'd never have to work again!In reality, as nice as the lads were, we were never going to be best mates. I'm only a year older than Davies, but I may as well have been 20 years older. They were teenagers destined for a millionaire lifestyle - quite literally - and I was wearing a Burtons pre-packed shirt and tie combo. Footballers and mere mortals just don't mix.

They answered all my questions, posed for photographs playing keepy-ups with an inflatable globe (world at their feet, see?) and didn't give much away – though Digger did say his younger brother always used to sign him for Man Utd on Championship Manager. But one man on the training pitch that day didn't conform to the footballer stereotype. While the rest of the squad gave assistant manager Paul Ashworth their undivided attention (Barry Fry stood on the sidelines, watching), one lank-haired squad member looked away, hands on hips, giving off the world weary demeanour of a hardened New York City Cop being given a dressing down by a fresh-from-college female HR advisor. Born in London in 1971, Dean Raymond Hooper was a late bloomer in the football world. He didn't get a gig at a pro club until he was 24. A trainee at Brentford, he jobbed around the likes of Hendon, Marlow, Hayes and Yeading (before they were one club) before being thrown a lifeline at Swindon Town. First-team chances for the tough-tackling right back were few and far between at the County Ground and so it was that Deano wound up on loan at London Road in 1997. The loan was a success, the fans took to him, but it wasn't until 1998 that Hooper made his move permanent. On the day that the teenage prodigies were supposed to be the star attraction, it was Hooper who caught the eye. A year into his Posh career, he looked every inch the old pro, seemingly shrugging off the advice of Ashworth – a boss only two years older than he was. After a few set-piece drills, Ashworth, standing by the corner taker, lost patience with Hooper, who was strolling around somewhere midway between the penalty area and halfway line. "You know you're supposed to be getting in the box without him seeing you, right?" asked Ashworth, voice raised, but still calm. "Oh yeah," said Hooper, nodding slowly, with more than a dash of lip. "I'm quite shrewd like that." Hooper then looked to the touchline, to my photographer and me, and rolled his eyes. He was playing to the crowd, albeit a small crowd. But whether he was playing in front of three men and a dog, or a crowd of 10,000, Hooper thrived on attention.

He wasn't the most gifted of footballers, but he gave 100%. Perhaps the years of toiling in non-league football had taught him that effort will be rewarded.

Hooper made close to 150 appearances and scored 2 goals for Posh before departing on a free transfer to Aldershot in 2002.

But during a generally pretty forgettable time for the club, Hooper left his mark – scoring his first Posh goal in the 9-1 demolition of Barnet, and playing in both legs of the Div 2 Play Off semi final (injury kept him out of the final). And in the decade since hardman Hooper left Posh, no-one else has made the right-back spot their own in quite the same way.

Jack Thorpe

Simon Davies

1993-2000
Appearances: 73
Goals: 6

You didn't need to be an expert to see from his very early Posh appearances that Simon Davies was a very special player. It helped of course that he had been coached by a genius, in the form of Kit Carson during his time at London Road. Indeed the club have Kit to thank for the fact that Simon followed him from Norwich City to Posh as a youngster.

Davies calmly authoritative midfield promptings were lapped up by a London Road crowd that had suffered some awful players masquerading as footballers during the early years of the Barry Fry dictatorship. He had the ability to pick a pass and get a shot on target even during the heat of a lower league game.

For me, his legendary PUFC moment came in August 1999 at the home of our bitter local rivals Northampton Town. Now, SixfingersFields is a shocking place and it is difficult to get any atmosphere going, but when Davies stepped up to rattle in the only goal of the game from 20 yards the Posh fans went crazy. Talking to the Peterborough Evening Telegraph in 2006, Davies said "It's still one of the best moments of my career and certainly the best goal because it meant so much to so many people.

"It was the only game against Northampton that I ever played in, but it was obvious in the build-up to the game that it was a huge occasion for the fans.

"We all knew that we had to produce in that match and thankfully we did. It was a passionate game on and off the pitch, but we deserved to win and the reaction from the fans afterwards was superb."

Davies left London Road to go to Spurs, along with Matthew Etherington. He has gone on to serve Spurs, Everton and Fulham in the Premier League, as well as gain over 50 caps for Wales. I love the fact that the win over Cobblers is still a career highlight for him. Altogether now....

"Who put the ball in the Cobblers net? Super Simon Davies Suuuuuper Suupper Si, Super Simon Davies"

Helgi Danielsson

1998-2003

Appearances: 40

Goals: 3

A Saturday evening in mid-November, 2006. Two University mates are on the sofa of their student house flicking through the various sports channels. It's an international weekend and after enjoying an afternoon of cheap lager and Jeff Stelling, England are boring their way to a 0-0 draw against some side from Eastern Europe. Seeking entertainment the students settle on a nondescript qualifying match involving two of Europe's minnows.

"Hold on – I recognise him," blurted one of the students.

"Who?" asked his non-Posh mate, intrigued.

"The guy coming on. He used to play for Posh."

A roll of the eyes. "Mate, according to you, everybody used to play for Posh. Hasn't Barry Fry signed every player outside of the Premiership for you at some point?"

"But this isn't like Dave Regis or Miguel De Souza. This guy is f***ing good."

The player coming off the Icelandic substitutes' bench went by the name of Helgi Valur Danielsson. Perhaps not the first name to spring to mind when considering players of Cult Hero status, but a player who is surely worthy of a claim. Danielsson was one of the better, more graceful players to line up in mid-field during Fry's reign - "not exactly hard" I hear you mutter - but throw into the mix that the club had players such as Simon Davies, Jimmy Bullard and Martyn O'Connor under his management and the fact that he seemed to sign at least one player a week over his decade or so in charge, then that is certainly praise indeed. Fry cannot take the credit for signing Danielsson however, and although he didn't come through the ranks from a particularly early age, he was certainly a product of the splendid Academy that the club boasted at the time.

"When I was seventeen I got in contact with an English agent who said he could get me some trials in England if I was interested," recalled the former Posh no.23, in an exclusive interview for this book. "The first of which happened to be at Posh, a club that I had never heard of but quickly found out played in the Third Division and had a good Academy set-up. I'm pretty sure that the club had never heard of me either and it was on the recommendation of my agent, and the fact that I had a few under-16 caps under my belt, that got me the trial. I came for a two weeks in September of 1998 and got to play an Under 19 Academy league game after only a week, against my favourite club, Liverpool, who fielded Steven Gerrard. The match finished 2-2 and after the game Paul Ashworth (Under-19 manager at the time) told me he wanted to sign me. After a few days' considerations and talks with my family, I signed a 2 year contract with Posh and moved to England."

The fact that Ashworth was so impressed with 'Helgs' is in itself a huge compliment. The Under-19 side had recently made club history by reaching the semi-finals of the FA Youth Cup. That side will always be remembered fondly by Posh fans given that it included the likes of 'Digger' and 'Mushy' – two of the best players ever to wear the blue who went on to play at the top level of English football for a decade.

"Although I came after all that I saw the newspaper articles and heard the stories from the players. I definitely got the feeling that they had done something fantastic and it gave the players involved a lot of confidence. I never actually played a game with Simon as he was already in the first team when I came to

Posh, and only a couple with Matthew (Etherington). There were some really good players in the youth team at that time and as a midfielder I always thought Matthew Gill, for one, was a fantastic player and I also looked up to Tony Shields and Anders Koogi.

"Ashworth and Aidy Boothroyd both coached me at Under-19 level and they were both excellent and they both showed that they believed in me as a player, even though I went through some rough patches. Later on John Morling, who was coaching the Under-17 side, became a good friend that helped me immensely and I even lived with him and his family for a while."

As if moving to a professional club in England was not fairytale enough for Helgi, he managed to secure a trial at AC Milan. The San Siro it wasn't to be but who needs that when you've got Ashton Gate.

"At the time of my Posh debut I remember being extremely nervous. I came on for about five minutes against Bristol City away and only managed to touch the ball a couple of times. I remember feeling like the tempo was extremely high but that was probably due to my anxiety."

Helgi does reflect on his time at Peterborough United with great affection. Posh are listed as his favourite football club on his Facebook page and he enjoys watching the team whenever he can.

"There were times when it was quite turbulent at the club, when we were fighting to stay in the league, when everyone wanted Fry out or when a coach got sacked and so on, but for the most part the atmosphere was good and I enjoyed coming to training every day. I think that most football clubs tend to have periods of turbulence and that it's simply a part of the job. It's certainly been no different in the clubs I've represented since."

There is one game that stands out for Helgi as his most magical occasion at London Road. Despite Leon McKenzie scoring a hat-trick, he was without doubt the best player on the pitch on a night when everything went right for him and the Posh.

"My most memorable match was definitely against Tranmere at home when I scored two goals and we won 5-0. Leon scored the other three goals and stole my limelight. It was a great night and I still remember that great feeling I had after the match.

"I only have good memories from the fans and they definitely stood by me during my time at the club. Interestingly, I've had some really good interaction with fans now, long after I left the club, and for me that is just fantastic. Just the fact that people remember me after all those years means that I must have made at least an impression on them and the club. The last game I saw at London Road was against Cardiff a couple of years ago when the Posh came from 4-0 down at half time to draw the game 4-4. One of the most amazing games I've ever witnessed live."

It's fair to say that Peterborough United Football Club is a very different place to the one Helgi left back in 2003. But it does go through one's mind: Wouldn't it be great to see the Icelandic star line up on the right-hand side of Darren Ferguson's diamond?

"I could see myself playing for Posh again, but I don't think it's very likely. The club has been run quite differently in recent years and success has followed. Playing in the championship is something I would like to try but I've only got a few more years in me and we'll just have to see what options pop up."

Jimmy Bullard

2001 - 2003
Appearances: 73
Goals: 14

A first look at Jimmy Bullard indicated that he would, disappointingly, be yet another failed Fry free transfer punt. You know the type: 'Posh Sign Ex-Premier League Star' and it turns out the player was in the youth team and the closest they got to a first-team appearance was sitting on the bench for a League Cup game.

Jimmy was pretty awful in his first couple of games and looked completely out of his depth. Skinny little legs and running about helplessly are my abiding memory of him. But then something clicked - he and Richard Forsyth complimented each other in a 'Tortoise and the Hare' partnership. Jimmy did all the running and was always available for a pass.

He then added thunderous shooting from outside the box to his repertoire and a legend was born. In a team battling gamely to stay in League One Jimmy took on an all-action role taking all the corners, free-kicks and even trying to be in charge of all throw-ins too. At time his speed of thought got him into trouble as the rest of the team just couldn't keep up with him.

Naturally his outstanding form in a poor team lead to plenty of interest from bigger, and richer clubs. Jimmy was sold for the criminally low sum of £275,000. The club was in turmoil as Peter Boizot to cope with the less than Corinthian modern game. Barry Fry was frozen out of the negotiations when his eye for an sell-on clause would've been invaluable. Jimmy moved to Wigan and has since racked up transfer fees of £2m and £5m in subsequent moves.

Posh also played a big part in his re-invention as one of the nations cheeky lovable football characters. The Posh Independent Supporters Association asked Jimmy to record a message for a function they were organising and the video of him trying, and repeatedly failing, to read a message from a cue-card became an internet sensation and introduced him to the wider public.

Tom Williams

2001-2002, 2004, 2007-2010
Appearances: 106
Goals: 4

If you were to look up the phrase 'fanny-merchant' in your football Profanisaurus you would probably find a photo of Tom Williams illustrating the definition. He is the quintessential modern footballer: always sports a zeitgiesty haircut, wears garish boots, a busty wife, amusingly monikered children and not nearly as talented as he thinks he is.

But, when he was on song he could be quite thrilling to watch. And what a left foot. Tom was a defender who wasn't that bothered about defending but loved dashing forward. His return to the club during Darren Ferguson's first spell in charge was a curious signing but ended up working out quite well.

In this second-spell at the club Tom made what I consider three significant contributions to our success. Firstly, that hack on Jack Lester as the Chesterfield striker bore down on goal. Williams had only been on the pitch for a minute when it happened and Posh were hanging on to a 2-1 lead. In a display of blatant gamesmanship that even a Portuguese international would've been proud of Williams took an age to leave the pitch antagonising the match officials and the Chesterfield penalty-taker. When the penalty was finally taken Joe Lewis saved it and Posh remained on course for promotion.

His second significant intervention came the following season as Posh chased promotion once again. Tom arrived as a second-half substitute as Posh struggled against Scunthorpe. The pitch in front of the South Stand was scorched as Tom got forward repeatedly and fired in cross after tempting cross. Scunthorpe had no answer to his devilish left foot and a baying London Road End. It was a crucial win as it kept us hot on the heels of Leicester and maintained the distance between us and our rivals Scunthorpe.

The third was his partnership with George Boyd. There were many right-backs driven to distraction by the pair. Do I mark Tom and give Boyd room or do I mark George and let Williams overlap? Very few teams had an answer and Posh prospered.

Tom Williams, bit of a tool but a part of one of the most thrillingly attacking Posh sides I've ever seen.

Paul Mitchell

Guy Branston

2004, 2006-2007
Appearances: 46
Goals: 2

At the time of writing, Guy Branston has played for 21 clubs during his 14 year career (on loan or permanently). This long list of clubs includes three spells at London Road (2 on loan, with 1 permanent stay). His no nonsense attitude, almost psychotic will to win, his determination to head the ball even when it is a foot off the ground with boots flying, made him a huge fans favourite during his spells at London Road. Guy was a poor mans version of Gaby Zakuani, he did exactly what it said on the tin – head it, kick it, tackle it. He was even given the captains armband during the 2006-7 season, in a bid to inspire his fellow players to get stuck in.

After loan spells at Rochdale and Wobblers, Guy was released from his PUFC contract in December 2007. He is yet another example of the London Road crowds adoration for a formidable central defender and sits in a long list (in reality at the bottom of the list..) containing the likes of Turner, Wile, McElhinney, Robinson and Zakuani.

Here is what Guy had to say when I caught up with him recently:

Your Proudest Posh moment?

Captaining the side, every time I did. I loved leading the lads into battle . Barry Fry made me captain when I came on loan from Rotherham . It was a good time and we stayed up that season in League one

Biggest disappointment?

Not getting in Darren Ferguson side. A very good manager I wanted to work for. I really wanted to stay ,but he was going with young players from Non league and he signed some really good players .Gutted to leave.

Best Barry Fry moment?

I did the deal for my contract in the betting shop in the ground. Me and Barry Fry would be in there a lot. When signing Barry Fry said if the horse wins I could get £50 more a week . And it did. That was an extra .And that was Barry Fry.

Best player you played with?

Boyd, I think you could just see that he could be who he wanted to be. And he has had a great time with Peterborough. Great player

And your feelings about Posh?

Love it . Its a place I got excited about going to . Training, games, just hanging around because there was always something going on .Remember I had there different times there and really enjoyed it. Hopefully I could come back as Manager one day.

George Boyd

2006 -
Appearances: 224
Goals: 64
*up until 30/10/11

There are very few superlatives that haven't been used to describe George Boyd. His natural skill and ability on a football is something that cannot be taught; it's something you either have or don't. The left winger has lit up London Road since his arrival in 2007 and there is now an argument to suggest he may well be the best player to have worn the blue Peterborough United.

At first it wasn't as easy to win the fans over though. Boyd came as a big money signing - £250,000 - the most any club had paid for a player from non-league football. A player without league experience but with potential. It was the marque signing to open the MacAnthony era. It was a gamble and one which certainly paid off.

Boyd arrived at Peterborough in January 2007 along with two other non-league hopefuls, Aaron McLean and Craig Mackail-Smith, who were looking to secure a career in league football. All three made their mark on Peterborough United history and continue to be held in high esteem, even though the "Mac-Attack" have gone elsewhere.

The left winger had been christened The White Pele by Stevenage fans and, therefore, had a lot to live up to at Posh. Boyd made his debut on a cold afternoon in Darlington where Peterborough lost 3-1. He looked a little lightweight but what he had was a killer instinct, a sensational first touch and the rare ability to look as if he had time on the ball wherever he received it. There was no doubt about it, from the first moment he put on a Posh shirt, the boy was talented.

A month later and Boyd was becoming a regular in the Peterborough United line-up. He had scored his first goal for the club in a comfortable win against Wrexham but it wasn't until The Posh played against Boston that he really announced his arrival and showed why Posh had splashed out such a sizable sum for him.

After falling behind to a poor Boston side Peterborough United needed a moment of brilliance to rescue them from an embarrassing defeat. Boyd was to provide it, coming off the bench he picked the ball up just inside his own half, cut inside, and unleashed an unstoppable volley into the top corner of the net. It was sensational, a piece of magic.

After establishing himself as the first name on the team sheet, the club's catalyst and being an inspiration in Peterborough United's promotion season from League Two – where he scored 15 goals – Boyd would go onto break a Posh record; he made 125 consecutive appearances beating Eric Steele's previous achievement of playing 124 times in a row. Quite remarkable for an outfield player to play so many times without getting injured, without losing form and without ever looking like he wanted a break.

He continued to progress as a player. In the 2008/2009 League One campaign he turned defenders inside-and-out, leaving a trail of bamboozled right-backs behind him. Few could get near him. It was the same in the Championship. Despite Posh's poor season, Boyd's performances were a positive and he scored a healthy amount of goals from midfield.

Despite there being times when it looked as if Boyd's time at Posh would be up, he still remains a Peterborough United player. The last of the Holy Trinity when many of us thought he would be the first to go. We have been privileged to watch him play for such a long period of time.

There have been some notable names that have made their way through Peterborough's ranks during my time; Simon Davies, Matthew Etherington and Jimmy Bullard have all played in the blue and white kit. Not one of these, however, can have had the impact Boyd had. For now, at least, Boyd remains a Peterborough United player and whilst he does Posh fans will continue to marvel at his brilliance.

John Verrall

Aaron Mclean

2006 - 2010
Appearances: 187
Goals: 84

Soon after purchasing Posh in 2006 Darragh MacAnthony asked manager Keith Alexander to point
him in the direction of the best striker and the best
player in non-league football. Aaron Mclean arrived
on loan shortly after and George Boyd arrived a few
months later. Thanks Keith

Aaron was an instant hit with the fans scoring on
his debut in the Football League Trophy and then a
few days later repeating the feat on his league debut.
The fans immediately warmed to his terrific on-field
attitude. He was positive, hard-working, a great motivator and had an eye for goal.

But I think what we'll remember most is his leap.
Prodigious doesn't really do it justice. At just 5ft 7in
he should've struggled against towering lower league
defenders but time and again they were caught out as
he won header after header.

And the leap was even more impressive if you saw
it close-up. In a pre-season game at Stamford I stood

behind the goal, just yards from the action, as he jumped for a cross. I would swear under oath that at the height of his leap his feet were above the cross-bar- just incredible

Soon after his loan move was made permanent in January 2007 he was joined at the club by Craig Mackail-Smith. Shortly after new manager Darren Feguson mused that the two might struggle to play in the same side - an opinion, that with hindsight, seems as ludicrous as such classic Posh management pronouncements as 'Ashley Vickers is the new Dave Robinson' and 'Dominic Green will play in the Premier League'.

The 'Mac-Attack' - a subset of the 'Holy Trinity' - became the most feared attack in the Football League. As described by Alan Swann: 'Mackail-Smith was the road-runner and Mclean was the smiling assassin. They could not stop scoring and the different threat they each posed proved impossible to contain for the average League Two Langmead trundler in the 2007/08 season. Aaron took the League Two Golden Boot as Posh surged to promotion. And the goals continued to flow the following season.

Despite a bit of a tantrum when Posh refused to let him join Wolves in the summer of 2008 and a further sulk when he was left out of the team to play Newcastle Aaron was a model professional.

An infectious smile and a willingness to do plenty of community work meant that he had a great rapport with the fans. I'm no fan-boy when it comes to individual players but one summer I saw him jogging, as part of his recover from a knee injury, over the Town Bridge. Sitting in my car I couldn't help myself and hooted and gave him the thumbs-up. I was rewarded with a huge grin and a cheery wave.

When he moved to Hull Posh made a huge profit on their initial £150,000 investment Thanks for the memories Aaron. And thanks once again Keith.

Darren Ferguson

2007 - 2009, 2010 -

We've had the Messiah, we've had the Son of God, the Holy Trinity and no end of Judas' but one of the most successful managers in our history hasn't yet been given a biblical moniker.

Fergie's arrival was something of a shock and the immediate response was that he'd only got the job beacuse of 'who his Dad is'. Later Darragh said he'd got the job because there was a 'connection' and "Darren was the only candidate who just wanted to talk about football and didn't want to talk about his bonus and getting a percentage of transfer profits.'

After a slow start his influence began to be felt. The playing department became much more professional and focussed. A fitness trainer arrived and Fergie fought hard to ensure that the players had proper facilities for training. Darragh was fully behind him and provided the finances to meet every request.

Fergie also defined a style of play. Ball on the floor with the emphasis on attack. Whilst the offical policy was 'young and hungry' he ensured that the midfield was anchored by an experienced pro with first Micah

Hyde and then Dean Keates providing the nous to go with the exuberance of youth. He inherited Grant McCann from Agent Johnson but after being unconvinced intially has made him the fulcrum of the team.

There was of course the break-up though. The exact facts and who said what to whom remain cloudy but Fergie's departure from the club didn't reflect well on either him or the club hierarchy. By the same token the mature way his return was handled reflected well on both Darragh and him.

Since, in Darragh's words, 'the band got back together' the results have been impressive. A third promotion under Fergie has been achieved and Posh continue to punch well above their weight in the Championship.

I've no idea how long he'll stay this but Darren Ferguson has given Posh fans some of the most exciting teams to watch in living memory. For that we should always be very grateful.

Craig Mackail-Smith

2007-2011
Appearances: 198
Goals: 99

There are a number of ways that players can gain hero status at a club. Some get it through their sheer drive, determination and commitment to the cause. Others gain the accolade by being a class above most others to represent the team and consistently showing a quality that surpasses what is expected. Craig Mackail-Smith did both.

The striker's start to life at Peterborough had been turbulent. His transfer from Dagenham and Redbridge had hardly been a smooth transition. Initially it seemed that he had rejected a move hoping, after seemingly being misled by an internet rumour, for a transfer to Sunderland instead. But finally it went through. Many weren't happy. But soon all our reservations were cast aside. He came as a non-league hopeful looking for a chance to prove himself. When this chance came along Craig Mackail-Smith was not the sort to let it slip.

Quick to establish himself as a regular starter Mackail-Smith instantly found his grove. Alongside Aaron McLean, the two created one of the deadliest attacking forces that Peterborough United fans had ever seen. But it was not just Mackail-Smith's wonderful goalscoring record that had endeared him to the London Road crowd; goals are only a minor part of his game. The term "a defender's nightmare" is used too often in football, yet the cliché simply doesn't do Mackail-Smith justice. For his marker wishes that he is a nightmare. Then they could wake-up, forget and move on. But for 90 minutes this nightmare does not go away. No matter where they go it is there. It is surrounding them and by the end many have given up, simply reduced to a nervous wreck.

It is this burning desire to run, press and hassle that endears Mackail-Smith to the fans so much. He plays as if he has one chance, every game seems like it is his last. From the stands it is tiring to watch. No matter how many times you see it, it remains startling. Nothing is a lost cause, and for 90 minutes Mackail-Smith seems as if he is on a one man mission. It was in his final season, though, that he became more than a hard working striker. He has become a wonderfully rounded player. He became a true Peterborough United legend.

Despite the hard-work, in previous years the jet-heeled striker had been guilty of missing too many gilt-edged chances. His goal-scoring record was impressive but question marks were raised whether he could make it the highest level where opportunities are harder to come by. These doubts are no longer. He most certainly can. Mackail-Smith is now clinical. He has added the one ingredient that was lacking. He is deadly in-front of goal. If he gets a chance, invariably, he scores it. Too often he has appeared a class above the opposition. Too often he has appeared a class-above his team mates.

Whilst the skill of players like George Boyd and Lee Tomlin is scintillating. From my time watching from London Road no-one has left me more in awe than Mackail-Smith. He isn't possessed the grace, poise and skill of some. But he just doesn't stop. The word give-up doesn't appear in his dictionary, no matter what is thrown at him Mackail-Smith doesn't quit. He inspires others to do the same and as a result Posh have shown great resilience in recent seasons.

After his transfer to Brighton, Posh fans still look on with interest at how he is doing. His career continues on an upwards trajectory too. He is fast becoming an established international striker, forcing his way into the Scotland starting line-up. From Dagenham, to Posh, to Brighton, to Scotland the features of his game have hardly changed but he is developed as a player, no doubt. And when tested on the toughest stage of the them all, against a wonderfully gifted Spain side, he still proved a handful – winning a penalty for his country. Posh fans looked on with pride then and with CMS' career continuing to move forward at startling pace it is likely that this feeling will be repeated a lot more in the future.

John Verrall

Charlie Lee

2007-2011
Appearances: 139
Goals: 16

Charlie 'Charlie Charles' Lee honestly believes that he is a brilliant box-to-box goal-scoring midfielder. The rest of us think he is a defender – of sorts.

Charlie's four seasons at Posh followed a distinctive pattern. Brilliant and energetic in pre-season he is in the starting line-up when the League kicks-off. But then he is a bit ineffectual and loses his place. This is followed by a month or three on the bench with either sporadic appearances or a spell out on loan. Then a defender is injured in January and Charlie fills in for them and plays magnificently until the end of the season.

2008/09 was a perfect example of this. Charlie had been distinctly average for five months but when pressed into service as an emergency centre-back, full-back, libero, sweeper he was magnificent. When Zak was sent off after a couple of minutes against the Cobblers Charlie was almost demonic in his defiance and his header secured an heroic backs-to-the-wall win. Then against Leicester he waltzed around two defenders into the area and lashed home the opening goal in a comfortable 2-0 victory. And then to top it all he scored the goal that clinched promotion at Colchester. Indeed he was so magnificent between February and May that the contribution of every other player – many of whom had been consistently good all season - was overlooked as Charlie took home every end-of-season award going including a BAFTA.

And yet at the beginning of the next season he was back on the bench again. Charlie repeated his heroic 2009 exploits as Posh surged to promotion again in 2011. Charlie was on the bench for the play-off final but when he was introduced in the second-half he marked his arrival with some fist-pumping, shouting and a karate kick to the midriff of the first Huddersfield player he came up against. I'd like to imagine that he said: "Believe in that you ****" to the stricken Huddersfield player as he waited for the ref to give him the inevitable booking.

Every squad needs a Charlie Lee and I'm glad he was around when we needed him.

Paul Mitchell

Shaun Batt

2008-2010
Appearances: 61
Goals: 4

Shaun Batt - a legend in the same way that Eddie the eagle is a legend.

I mainly remember Shaun Batt being so, so bad that he turned out quite good. Mainly used as an impact sub he came on and just ran. And that's all he could really do, before inevitably falling over. Or doing something unbelievably good. On purpose? I have no idea, taking it past three players and finally skying his shot a good 20 yards over the bar.

Or the time when he came on against Millwall back in our League One promotion season he was so ineffectual he may as well not have been there. I remember thinking to myself; how has he made it into professional football as he fell over for the third time.

Although he had moments of magic such as when he won a penalty against Derby followed by a 25-larder against Palace live on Sky. And finally his magic goal against Middlesbrough where he chested and volleyed brilliantly over Brad Jones. I will never forget that.

I'm glad we let him go for £300,000 of great profit, considering he cost us about £15,000 I think. He was probably chuffed to leave as Millwall were going up and we were going straight back down.

James Lorimer

Gabriel Zakuani

2008 -
Appearances: 117*
Goals: 4*
*Up until 30/10/11

Zak has a special place in the heart of many Posh fans. He is the very epitome of the player that gives his all and is, right up there in the "never give up" category at London Road, alongside the likes of Rigby and Halsall.

Zak arrived at London Road on loan in - what would turn out to be - the 2008/9 promotion from League One season. After settling in and becoming a firm fans and managerial favourite he signed permanently for PUFC in January 2009, and has never looked back.

At least once a game, Zak puts his head and body on the line trying to prevent a shot on goal, or alternatively he is throwing one of his long legs into a challenge to protect his goal. A man that truly loves the dark arts of defending, Zak was the first Posh player to become a twitter phenomenon with his #EverydayImTackling.

Since the return of Darren Ferguson, we have also seen a huge improvement in Zaks much maligned passing ability. The man just loves a battle, whether that be through the awful 2008/9 Championship season or through months of the 2011/12 season when he played on with a broken toe and multiple pain-killing injections. A true hero of the London Road End.

Grant McCann

2010 -

Appearances: 57*

Goals: 19*

*up until 30/10/11

Curling, swerving, dipping and crashing into the back of the net. This wasn't just a goal. This was confirmation. This was promotion. As Grant McCann lined up a free-kick, 20 yards from goal, there was a certain expectation around Old Trafford that the ball would hit the back of the net. That distance has become known among Posh fans as 'Grant McCann range'.

McCann's leadership through the play-offs will mean he will always be remembered fondly around London Road. This goal was the icing on the cake for Posh, this was the culmination of the season and this was McCann's reward for his efforts in the three most high pressure games in Posh's recent history. McCann wore the armband for Posh for the majority of the season, but throughout the play-offs he epitomised the meaning of being a captain. The Northern Ireland international was the embodiment of guts, determination and leadership.

McCann was the coolest person in Stadium:MK when he stepped up to take that penalty. It was not an exaggeration to say that Posh's play-off ambitions rested on his kick from twelve yards. At 3-1 down, with 10 men, with a sizeable amount of the match to be played and with MK Dons on top it seemed that Posh's promotion ambitions were over. Yet, this spot-kick provided Peterborough United with a route into the tie. The nerves were tangible, but McCann simply went through his normal routine - taking two extended steps to the right of the ball – and slotted the ball into the back of the net. The most difficult of tasks, given the circumstances, made to look like the easiest.

Then at London Road, with Posh 3-2 down on aggregate and needing someone to take the game by the scruff of the neck and drive them forward, he was that man. He set up the comeback. Spotting David Martin, the MK Dons goalkeeper, out of position and expecting a cross he delicately clipped a free-kick over the wall and into the corner of the net. From that moment, you got the sense that it was going to be Posh's night.

Of course, McCann will not only be remembered for his efforts in the play-offs. He is one of the most technically gifted central midfielders to ever wear the blue-shirt. With a quite magnificent left-foot, he has an ability with a football that very few players possess. He can smash a football into the back of the net from 30 yards, but also has the quality to thread the ball through the eye of a needle to a team-mate. The fact he has over 25 assists and 17 goals in less than 50 appearances for Peterborough United is testament to this.

Under Gary Johnson, Grant McCann was a good player. Under Darren Ferguson he is the fulcrum of the team. Ferguson, indeed, changed Posh's style – from a 2 man central midfield pairing, to having a trio of players in the middle of the park – just to suit McCann. He has become one of the integral parts of Posh's passing style, sitting at the base of the diamond, he is the player who dictates the play. When McCann plays well, invariably, Peterborough United play well.

Many players endear themselves to the fans because of their never-say-die attitude, or because of their incredible efforts but McCann has won the Posh crowd over in a different way. Because of his ability with a football at his feet. Before the play-offs McCann would have been recognised as an excellent midfielder. But, after three glorious moments in two weeks, he has become an unforgettable piece of Peterborough United folklore.

Ryan Bennett

2009 -

Appearances: 77*

Goals: 6*

* up until 30/10/11

At the time of writing (October 2011), Bennett remains the clubs record signing at around £500,000 and a newly crowned England U21 International. Bennett has the cool, calm, match reading qualities of Alan Hansen, and many judges feel that he will make the Premier League, with or without Posh in the very near future.

Bennett was Ferguson's last signing in his first reign at the club, and indeed appeared to be down the pecking order during the calamitous reign of Gary Johnson. When Ferguson returned, he returned Bennett to the starting line-up and was rewarded with a series of stunning central defensive performances.

As Darragh MacAnthony commented to the Standing On The Glebe podcast (available free on iTunes) in August 2011: "if Leicester are prepared to pay £4M for Matt Mills, the Reading defender, what will Benno be worth after a good season in the Championship?"

Paul Taylor

2011 -

Appearances: 15*

Goals: 4*

* up until 30/10/11

As I write this (August 2011), I have absolutely no idea whether Paul Taylor will go on and become a first team regular for PUFC. However, on a wet Wednesday evening this week at The New Den he produced one of the best substitute appearances that I have ever seen. Coming on with the team 2-0 down to a dogged and physical Millwall side, he changed the game immediately with his direct running and close control. The game was over, gone, lost at 2-0; but then Taylor set up Lee Frecklington and suddenly it was 2-1. Taylor then ran himself into the ground chasing around the park searching out the ball and then heading towards the Millwall goal whenever he got hold of it. At this point it is worth reminding ourselves that Taylor is a 23yr old who got kicked out of Chester City FC for drug use and then went to play in the Belgium 5th tier before being rescued by Darren Ferguson. For the equalising goal in this Champion-ship fixture, he picked up the ball on the left hand side, skids inside one defender and sends a shot along the turf into the bottom corner. The 400 odd Posh fans high up in the stand go absolutely bonkers at a point gained and a new cult hero born.

London Road

I am sure that all football fans think that their clubs ground is special, but for me, on certain very special occasions, London Road can be the best place on earth.

Since I started attending London Road in 1983, the place has always felt old. Even the addition of the new all-seater Glebe stand in the mid 1990's, simply served to highlight how decrepit the Main Stand and London Road End were - and still are.

However, it is a home that has served the club, and its' fans well over the years, and has leant itself to some amazing atmospheres. We are, let's face it, not the biggest or loudest set of supporters in the land, but given the right occasion we can make a 'helluva racket'. Every fan will have their special London Road memories. Many who are old enough to remember will hark back to May 1974 and the visit of Gilling-ham, which saw 17,569 squeeze into the ground.

Some will go even further back, to the clubs first ever football league game, at home to Wrexham in August 1960, when again over 17,000 crammed onto the terraces. For me, there is something about a game at London Road under the perennially dull floodlights that can spark a partisan atmosphere. My two favourite examples would be:

v Liverpool in the League Cup, 3rd December 1991. The crowd came expecting a good sing-song maybe a clattering Mick Halsall tackle for one of the Liverpool artisans and a hopefully narrow defeat. What we got was a goalkeeping mistake resulting in a 1-0 win, and an atmosphere that inspired the players forward. The noise and whistling, imploring the referee to blow the final whistle seemed to reverberate round the corrugated iron roof of the London Road End, making a wall of noise. The explosion of jumping around and celebrating would not be matched at London Road for almost 20 years....

v MK Dons, League One Play-Off Semi Final Second Leg, 19th May 2011. Grant McCann's penalty at Stadium MK had meant that we got away from the soulless, concrete monstrosity with only a narrow 3-2 defeat, despite not playing well. The four days between the away and home leg saw the fans forums and the local press come into their own, in generating an incredible level of anticipation. On the night, prior to kick off, the club got it spot on with many of the players featured in this book, coming out onto the pitch to hail their adoring public. The bawling of the PUFC anthems of Posh We Are and The Last Waltz was a raucous indication to the small MK following of what was to come. The team performed brilliantly on the pitch to win the game 2-0, the crowd did not stop singing and roaring them on to victory. At the end, another very special moment, with the crowd spilling onto the pitch to hail a play-off semi final win, and a trip to Old Trafford that was to end with promotion and tears of joy - maybe that was just me though?